WITHDRAWN

FARM LABOR ORGANIZING

D1559932

ILR PAPERBACK NUMBER 21

FARM LABOR ORGANIZING

TRENDS & PROSPECTS

MARALYN EDID

ILR PRESS
ITHACA, NEW YORK

For Larry, Aaron, and Maia

HD
6515
. A29
E34
1994

Copyright©1994 by Cornell University

Library of Congress Cataloging-in-Publication Data

Edid, Maralyn, 1950–
Farm labor organizing: trends and prospects / Maralyn Edid.
p.   cm. — (ILR paperback: no. 21)
Includes bibliographical references and index.
ISBN 0-87546-321-5 (pbk.: acid-free paper)
1. Trade-unions—Agricultural laborers—United States.   2. Trade-unions—Agricultural laborers—California.   3. Trade-unions—United States—Organizing.   4. Trade-unions—California—Organizing.
5. Collective bargaining—Agriculture—United States.   6. Collective bargaining—Agriculture—California.   I. Title.   II. Series.
HD6515.A29E34   1994
331.88'13'0973—dc20   94-9010

Copies may be ordered through bookstores or directly from

ILR Press
School of Industrial and Labor Relations
Cornell University
Ithaca, NY 14853-3901

Printed on acid-free paper in the United States of America

5   4   3   2   1

Contents

Acknowledgments

This book has been in process for a long time. I suppose its roots could be traced to the years I spent on kibbutzim in Israel, where I performed my fair share of agricultural labor, albeit under conditions far more humane and ennobling than those experienced by migrant and seasonal farmworkers in the United States during the waning years of the twentieth century. I suppose it could also be traced to my great-uncle, an early leader of the International Ladies' Garment Workers' Union in the New York City area, and to my grandparents, who were stalwart members of "the ILG" for years.

But more directly, the book is the outgrowth of a report I undertook for the New York State Department of Labor when I first joined the Extension Division of the New York State School of Industrial and Labor Relations (ILR) at Cornell University in June 1990. At the time, the state was seeking policy guidance from Cornell about whether to extend to farmworkers the protected right to organize and bargain collectively over terms and conditions of employment. The state's labor department funded a year-long project that involved an interdisciplinary task force of faculty representatives from ILR, the New York State College of Agriculture and Life Sciences, and the New York State College of Human Ecology, all based at Cornell. We completed our work in May 1991 with a recommendation that the state amend the New York State Labor Relations Act to remove language that specifically excludes farmworkers from its safeguards and protections. I was the primary researcher and author of the final report, "Agricultural Labor Markets in New York State and Implications for Labor Policy."

Parts of the book also derive from testimony and a paper I prepared for the Commission on Agricultural Workers during the summer of 1991. Authorized by Congress to assess the effect on agriculture of the Immigration Reform and Control Act of 1986 (IRCA), the Commission held a series of hearings and workshops throughout the country in 1990 and 1991. I was invited to testify at a workshop about the impact of IRCA on farmworkers' ability to organize. The additional research I undertook for this assignment informed key sections of the finished manuscript.

Many people deserve a round of applause and a hearty "thank you" for their cooperation, support, and patience. In particular, I would like to thank my publisher, Fran Benson, for her gentle reminders that this project should come to closure, and the two outside readers, John Leggett and Linda Majka, for the insightful comments that prompted me to read more and think bigger. I would also like to thank my colleagues at ILR, especially Associate Dean and Director of Extension Ron Seeber, and extension associates at Programs for Employment and Workplace Systems, who generously provided the mental space and time I needed to complete the work. Thanks, too, to Charlie Horwitz and Debra Sabatini Dwyer, who were critical friends at the end, and to Monica Heppel for including me in the commission's work. Scores of people spent countless hours talking with me about farmworkers, farming, history, immigration, laws, and unions. Those who agreed to be so named are listed in the back of the book, and to you and all my anonymous sources I again say, thank you.

And finally, there is my family.

Note on Methodology and Sources

I was trained as a journalist long before I ever began to think or write about labor issues in a more academic vein. As a result, the book reflects my particular combination of skills and inclinations. I read widely and talked to anyone I could locate. What I discovered was that many facts and conclusions about the farm labor force and farmworker collective bargaining were "common knowledge," in that they could not be easily traced to any particular source. In assembling my materials, however, I tried to stay true to the written sources and supplied attributions when appropriate. Information gathered through conversations became part of my general store of knowledge and were simply incorporated into the text without attribution. I have appended a complete bibliography, supplying even those references not specifically cited in the book, so that anyone eager to undertake their own education can begin with the list I assembled. I have also provided a list of almost everyone I interviewed. It is the breadth of this reporting that made the topic come alive for me, and will, I hope, do the same for the reader.

1. Introducing the Farmworkers

Labor unions are on the defensive these days. Often maligned by employers and workers for the erosion of America's manufacturing base, for the loss of competitiveness and jobs to lower-cost and (perceived) higher-quality foreign producers, the union movement has seen its stature flag and its numbers decline. Union membership may still promise above-average wages and generous benefits, but a string of recessions and the awakening of other national economies has caused a fundamental realignment of power on the world's economic stage and a loss of leverage for organized labor.

Although public opinion surveys show support for the idea of unions and their instrumental role in workplace governance (Weiler 1990:299), unions are also viewed as corrupt, greedy, authoritarian, and elitist (BNA 1985:11). In a fit of historical forgetfulness or ignorance or fear, many American workers spurn the very organizations born of the conviction that employees need a collective voice, a say in matters that affect their work lives, some protection against the capricious and arbitrary control of employers.

Maybe American workers believe unions have failed them. Maybe they are cowed by management teams that threaten to ship jobs elsewhere, that overpower and outmaneuver "big labor" in high-stakes, highly public contract negotiations. And maybe, just maybe, they take for granted their right to form unions and bargain collectively and feel no compelling need to act on it.

Now consider American farmworkers. They do not even have the statutory protection to embrace or reject a union, to be represented

1

by colleagues of their own choosing. Farmworkers are one of the few occupational groups in the United States that have no recognized legal right to organize and bargain collectively over terms and conditions of employment. Farmworkers, along with domestic workers and people employed by a parent or spouse, are specifically excluded from the National Labor Relations Act (NLRA). Passed in 1935 as a critical component of President Franklin D. Roosevelt's New Deal, the act recognizes workers' fundamental and pre-existing right to form unions and bargain over terms and conditions of employment. Right up front, in Section 1, the NLRA declares federal policy to be that of encouraging the practice of collective bargaining. The statute also established the National Labor Relations Board (NLRB) to interpret and implement provisions of the act.

The NLRA covers the vast majority of nonmanagerial private sector workers in the United States. Some people, such as independent contractors and supervisors, were excluded by the 1947 Taft-Hartley amendments. Employees of small businesses are denied the act's protections by virtue of revenue-based jurisdictional standards set by the NLRB. Postal workers and employees of nonprofit hospitals were brought under the act's aegis during the 1970s through legislation and additional amendments. Railroad workers are covered by the Railway Labor Act, passed nine years before the NLRA and amended in 1936 to include airline employees.

Government workers, by and large, also enjoy the right to organize and bargain collectively. Federal employees have been allowed to bargain over working conditions (but not wages) since 1962, when President John F. Kennedy issued Executive Order 10988. Two dozen states have granted comprehensive bargaining rights to public employees, the most recent being New Mexico, which bucked the current trend toward restricting workers' rights when it enacted collective bargaining legislation in 1992.

What Unions Have Wrought

Although only a minority of the American work force has ever been or is currently unionized (35 percent at the peak in 1954 and 16 percent in 1992), the mere existence of collective bargaining laws has had a salutary and stabilizing impact on the tone and content of

labor-management relations in this country. The NLRA was enacted after more than a decade of turbulence and upheaval in the
nation's factories. Violent strikes, sitdowns, beatings, sabotage,
strikebreaking, and court-ordered injunctions against union activists and sympathizers loomed large on the industrial scene.

It finally became apparent that such disruptions not only inter-
fered with production and commerce, they also threatened the
social, political, and economic order. And so the NLRA was conceived. Supporters of the act had high expectations for the new law.
They were convinced the act would restore and thus promote industrial peace, ensure the viability of the established order, and guarantee a form of industrial democracy that would reinforce and
mirror America's political democracy.

With the statute firmly in place, labor and management could
finally play by a known and codified set of rules. Provisions of the
act covered union organizing campaigns, procedures for holding
representation elections, union recognition, employer unfair labor
practices, strikes and work stoppages, and remedies. After a while,
a type of social contract evolved between employers and unions,
whereby management accepted the reality and necessity of organized labor and labor accepted the reality and durability of America's market economy (Marshall 1987:114). From that time forward,
most contract negotiations and labor disputes have been settled
amicably, without strikes, without lost work time, and without
resort to overburdened administrative and judicial systems.

As unions grew in number and strength during and immediately
following World War II, terms and conditions of employment for
organized workers improved dramatically. Contract provisions
guarding employees against arbitrary treatment by employers and
first-line supervisors, in the form of grievance procedures, seniority
clauses, and strict job classification schemes, were pivotal early
victories for the union movement. The war era wage-stabilization
period prompted many unions to suppress their monetary goals
and bargain instead for shift premiums and paid vacations and
holidays, for pensions and health and welfare plans, with the large
and powerful unions in mining, auto, steel, and textiles playing
leadership roles in these efforts. In 1949, an NLRB ruling that was
affirmed by the federal courts made health and welfare packages
mandatory subjects of bargaining (Slichter, Healy, and Livernash
1960:375, 403, 404).

Organized labor did not just coast on these achievements. It moved forward with other innovations, such as the 1948 agreement between the United Auto Workers (UAW) and General Motors Corporation, which inaugurated the practice of awarding annual wage increases based on average productivity gains (steady for years at 2 percent to 3 percent) and cost-of-living adjustments (COLA) as a hedge against inflation. Over the next two decades, the so-called "annual improvement factor" and COLA clauses were incorporated into many union contracts. The union movement also pressured industries with numerous small employers and casual employment patterns to provide pensions through multi-employer plans that were jointly controlled by labor and management. And the movement successfully lobbied legislators and policy makers for a raft of social welfare legislation ranging from aid to education to civil rights.

Fringe benefits and other hallmarks of collective bargaining quickly spread beyond the unionized sector. Managers at many companies, determined to resist union organizing drives, adopted "progressive" personnel and pay practices. By the mid-1950s, one study estimated that more than 50 percent of American wage and salary workers were covered by employer-provided hospitalization and surgical insurance and more than 30 percent of the workforce enjoyed some kind of retirement plan. Union members, however, were more likely to be party to these arrangements: about three-quarters of all organized workers boasted health and welfare benefits and about half of all organized workers were entitled to pensions (Slichter, Healy, and Livernash:376, 404).

Today, most American workers earn a living wage and receive such benefits as health insurance, disability and accident insurance, paid vacations and holidays, and retirement plans. Workers are entitled to at least one day of rest each week and receive premium pay for overtime hours. There are health and safety laws, civil rights laws, and child labor laws. Working conditions are generally tolerable and many employers treat employees with dignity and respect. Although a distressing number of companies have been shutting down operations and laying off workers, demanding wage cuts and retracting benefits once thought sacrosanct, exploiting undocumented and immigrant workers in sweatshops and low-pay, part-time jobs that offer no health and welfare plans, the majority of American workers are better off than they were fifty or sixty years ago, when benefit packages were virtually unknown and employees were regarded as little more than chattel.

... And Then There Are the Farmworkers

Labor relations in agriculture, by contrast, have been relatively immune to these forces. Almost two-thirds of the labor on American farms is performed by owner/operators and unpaid family members, making the norms of employer-employee interactions immaterial. A small group of farmworkers and many farm supervisors and marketing specialists hold permanent full-time jobs, earn moderate incomes, receive fringe benefits, live in adequate housing, and enjoy the community's respect.

Despite some legal and social reforms, living and working conditions for seasonal and migrant workers—those who follow the harvest or take a series of seasonal jobs in their own locales—have changed little since the 1930s. Successful and enduring unions, the traditional vehicle for worker self-help in this country, have not taken firm root in the farm sector. One consequence of this void is that the drudgery and insecurity of farmworkers' lives in the United States closely parallels the lives of rural and urban workers in many developing countries.

Consider, for example, farmworkers' large-scale migrancy: workers and their families trek across state and international borders year in and year out in search of work that may last a few days or maybe a few months. Migrant and seasonal farmworkers are plagued by chronic health problems, including diabetes, hypertension, infectious parasites, extraordinarily high rates of tuberculosis and cancer, and rising levels of HIV infection (Commission on Security and Cooperation in Europe 1993:15, 36, 42). The average lifespan of a farmworker is forty-nine years, just 67 percent of the U.S. average of seventy-three years (Commission on Security and Cooperation in Europe 1993:99). Many migrant and seasonal workers endure all manner of indignities, ranging from sexual abuse of women workers to the presence of guard dogs where people live and work, to supervision by gun, to racial discrimination and social isolation. Some farmworkers are kept in a form of peonage and are deeply in debt to unscrupulous employers or labor contractors, the middlemen who recruit and manage work crews.

Migrant and seasonal workers' financial circumstances are equally distressing. Wages barely float above the federal minimum of $4.25 an hour and average annual incomes posit most families well below the official poverty line (Commission on Agricultural Workers 1992:101). Migrant and seasonal workers have few defenses against the inevitable periods of unemployment in the off season or the unpredictable but recurrent bouts of underemployment at the height of the season. Their savings are meager or nonexistent, their skills are not easily transferred to nonagricultural work, their eligibility for state or federally supported social services is limited or unrecognized.

Certainly many farm employers treat workers appropriately. They abide by federal and state regulations concerning health and safety, compensation, insurance, and housing. They take care to recruit the number of workers they actually need and try to manage the work load to keep people gainfully employed for the longest period possible. Some make sure their employees get medical attention, take them shopping in town, know each worker and his or her family by name. On parts of the East Coast, where growers typically supply housing for their seasonal employees, some do provide satisfactory quarters, replete with washing machines and full kitchens.

But these relatively felicitous conditions are not the norm. Whether they live in town or in grower-owned camps, many migrant and seasonal workers are forced into overcrowded and substandard housing that lacks the bare necessities, like plumbing or heat or window screens. Male farmworkers in California have been known to pay rent of three hundred dollars a month for the right to sleep on the floor of a trailer with fourteen or fifteen coworkers. Thousands of farmworkers are illegally exposed to pesticides, denied access to (or have no right to expect) toilets and potable water in the fields, and transported to and from work by drunk, uninsured, or unlicensed drivers in rickety old vehicles. Many find employment with unethical growers or labor contractors who make intolerable demands on their time and bodies and then take unexplained and fraudulent deductions from their weekly pay. All too often the "boss" neglects to make required social security payments or pays all working family members in the father's name, thus denying each individual their eventual right to their own meager pension and minimizing the number of paid "man days" in order to limit the grower's exposure to federal and state protective labor laws (Commission on Security and Cooperation in Europe 1993 :33, 98–99).

Farmworker families subsist at a level of health and welfare that most Americans would consider intolerable. Medical care is usually hard to find and harder still to get to. Workers tend to let problems fester until they become unbearably severe, partly because they cannot afford to take time off to seek medical care, partly because they lack necessary transportation, partly because there are too few clinics and too few medical practitioners, and partly because cultural and economic barriers constrain their use of the medical system. Day care for many toddlers means accompanying parents to the fields or being left unattended in the family's shack.

Education for farmworker children is spotty. School enrollment is low and the drop-out rate is high: 45 percent for migrant children compared to 25 percent nationally (Commission on Security and Cooperation in Europe 1993:99). For many youngsters schooling yields to the family's need to move on, to the discomfort of sitting in class with younger students whose education is not so frequently interrupted, to the apathy and occasional hostility of the local school administration, and to the imperative of income-generating labor in the fields.

Indeed, child labor on American farms is a serious and scandalous problem. Applicable laws are controlled by the federal and state governments and represent a patchwork of regulations and safeguards, most of which make special allowances for, and are more lenient toward, farmwork. According to the United Farm Workers of America (UFW), the California-based farm labor union founded by the late Cesar Chavez, there are 800,000 children performing agricultural work in this country (Commission on Security and Cooperation in Europe 1993:97).

Conditions are so deplorable that the Commission on Security and Cooperation in Europe, which was established in 1975 by the Helsinki Final Act to monitor and encourage human rights compliance around the world, decided to investigate the plight of migrant and seasonal farmworkers in America. Beginning in December 1991 and extending through April 1993, the commission staff engaged in fact-finding investigations and held a series of public hearings. The Helsinki Commission, as it is commonly known, concluded its study with a series of recommendations that called for reform and stricter enforcement of existing labor laws that affect farmworkers, coordination among governmental agencies and provision of additional services for the relevant population, enhanced health and safety measures, and stronger efforts to keep children out of the fields and in the schools.

Farmwork ranks alongside mining and construction as one of the three most dangerous occupations in the United States. American society, however, provides no safety net and no rewards for the men, women, and children who are paid to cultivate the land and harvest our food. Government regulations are too few and too scantily enforced, numerous laws and regulations exclude farmworkers from their protective umbrella, and different states promulgate different minimal standards for the workplace. Farm employers, who are well-insulated by a chronic surplus of labor, have little incentive to raise wages, improve working conditions, or strive for better rapport with employees. Our callous treatment of, and dispassionate attitude toward, migrant and seasonal farmworkers is a national shame.

An Immigrant Work Force

It is the migrant and seasonal workers, found almost exclusively on labor-intensive fruit, vegetable, and horticultural farms, who suffer the worst features of the farm labor system. These workers constitute the bulk of the seasonal farm work force in the United States and claim 40 percent of the agricultural wage bill (Commission on Agricultural Workers 1992:2). Accurate and credible data on the farmworker population is nonexistent, although government and academic estimates put the count of migrant and seasonal workers at anywhere from one million to four million people, including dependents (*New York Times*:Feb. 24, 1992). An unknown proportion of this population continues to be only temporarily and seasonally attached to the farm labor force. Most workers, however, maintain long-term attachments to agriculture despite occasional forays into nonfarm employment (Commission on Agricultural Workers 1992:77).

Growers' ever-present fears of potential labor shortages have largely gone unrealized. For years, the supply of farm labor has been continuously replenished by waves of immigrants seeking financial and political haven in this country. The vast majority of migrant and seasonal workers now come from Mexico or Central America. Recent studies put the share of immigrants in the farm labor force at about 83 percent in California, Texas, Florida, and the Northwest but only 36 percent in the Midwest and on the East Coast. Government estimates of the number of illegal aliens or undocumented immigrants working in nonsupervisory agricultural jobs range from zero in the lower Rio Grande Valley to a high of 36 percent in central California. The Commission on Agricultural Workers, created by the Immigration Reform and Control Act of 1986 (IRCA) to study the law's effect on agriculture, says a reasonable mid-range estimate based on its own case studies is that 25 percent of the farm labor force is comprised of undocumented workers. (The number provided in the Department of Labor–sponsored study for the Rio Grande Valley sounds peculiar, given its proximity to the Mexican border. But there may be a plausible explanation. The commission reports that undocumented workers in Yuma County, Arizona, for example, are scarce primarily because many workers legally commute over the border to take advantage of less expensive housing in Mexico and then receive free, grower-provided transportation between the border and the fields [Commission on Agricultural Workers 1992:73, 89].

The immigrant character of the total paid farm labor force is so pronounced that the share of native born American farmworkers, now about 40 percent of the total, is shrinking rapidly (Mines, Gabbard, and Samardick 1992:642). The Midwest remains one of the few regions that still attracts a sizable domestic labor force and the East Coast continues to rely on a large proportion of Afro-American, Jamaican, and Haitian workers (Kissam and Griffith 1991:1:13, 25). But with the persistence of immigration and IRCA's amnesty program, which granted legal status to more than one million formerly undocumented farmworkers, foreign-born workers from Mexico, other Central American countries, and the Caribbean are pioneering into new areas and displacing their American peers.

Until 1992, the trend toward an immigrant-dominated workforce seemed further reinforced by the H-2A program. First established in 1952 by the Immigration and Nationality Act, the H-2 program (renamed H-2A with the passage of IRCA) allowed the importation of nonimmigrant contract workers to alleviate agricultural labor shortages as certified by the U.S. Department of Labor (DOL). In recent years more than 26,000 workers entered the United States annually for temporary jobs picking apples, irrigating, sheepherding, logging, cutting sugarcane, and performing other miscellaneous tasks. Slightly less than half the workers held contracts with the Florida sugarcane plantations and well over one-quarter were imported to work the apple orchards of the East Coast.

Controversy has long surrounded this program. The DOL is supposed to certify that no domestic workers are available and that the wages and working conditions offered contract workers will not adversely affect "similarly employed" domestic workers. Based on local surveys by the DOL and the U.S. Department of Agriculture, an adverse effect wage rate (AEWR) is set and the prevailing wage determined. Employers must pay their H-2A and domestic workers at least the highest rate established by the AEWR, the prevailing wage for the crop activity in the area, or the federal or state minimum wage. The federal government also establishes minimum standards for housing.

Critics allege the H-2A program does have an adverse effect on domestic workers, despite its contrary intent. They say it is too easy for growers to secure the necessary certification and thus not even bother to try filling the slots with domestic workers. The result of adding still more workers to an already oversupplied labor pool, critics charge, is that wages and benefits for domestic workers are further suppressed. H-2A opponents also contend that growers prefer contract workers because they are perceived to be more productive and seem less willing to complain about unjust wages and working conditions. In response, proponents argue that growers cannot find willing and capable domestic workers and that government standards for wages, benefits, and working conditions actually improve conditions for nearby domestic workers.

Farmworker advocates have filed numerous complaints and lawsuits challenging DOL certifications or implementation of other parts of the program. The cost and hassle of defending these cases is high and a number of growers are scaling back requests to import foreign workers. In 1992 the total number of certified jobs dropped to 18,800, from the 1989 high of 26,600, with only a fraction of the former 10,000 or so sought by and granted to sugarcane growers in Florida. Growers there are not hiring more domestic workers, however, but are turning to mechanical harvesting instead.

Farmworker Powerlessness

Despite growers' and consumers' near-total dependence on migrant and seasonal farmworkers, these people remain a marginal group in American society. Their modest numbers, racial and ethnic composition, and low status in the occupational hierarchy make them relatively powerless and vulnerable, consigned to the bottom of the socioeconomic ladder. Limited educational attainment, lack of transferable job skills, language, and cultural factors all inhibit their assimilation into the mainstream. Farm laborers have few staunch allies or advocates save for a handful of committed church groups, attorneys, and other professionals who work for migrant-centered social service agencies. Because farmworkers do not often speak out for themselves, legislators and regulators take little notice.

Sporadic efforts by mainstream political and social allies to improve farmworkers' lives have largely failed. Reforms instituted during the 1970s brought employees of the largest farms into the unemployment insurance system and established federal programs in health, child care, education, housing, legal services, and job training. Today, for example, the federal government spends about $500 million a year on education for children of farmworker families, for health care and job training (Commission on Security and Cooperation in Europe 1993:36).

But apart from these minimal programs, reformers have been stymied at nearly every turn by farmers and corporate agricultural interests whose powerful lobbies in the national and state capitals have long argued vociferously and triumphantly for agricultural exceptionalism. Seasonality, vulnerability to nature, make-or-break harvests, and an intensely competitive industry structure were, and still are, promoted as reasons why farming should be treated differently from other kinds of economic enterprises. Imports of basic and exotic fruits and vegetables from Mexico began to surge in the early 1980s, and the threat of still more imports from highly productive and lower-cost foreign producers only adds to the urgency of growers' appeals. Over the years, farmers' ongoing campaign has netted them a variety of crop subsidies, cheap credit, government-supported research, and exemptions or special treatment from a host of protective labor laws and regulations, including those concerning health and safety, social insurance, and collective bargaining.

Farming is certainly a risky venture and nurturing a strong agri-cultural sector is certainly a national priority. In the process of accommodating growers' financial and scientific needs, however, we apparently lost sight of the human factor. Policy makers and the public seem relatively unconcerned about the plight of migrant and seasonal farmworkers. Few Americans are fully cognizant of the conditions under which farm employees live and work, of the manual effort involved in the cultivation and harvest of food. Although there have been several brief interregnums when farm-workers were at the forefront of the nation's consciousness, little positive change or permanent improvement in their lives resulted.

In the pre–World War II years, public concern was momentarily aroused by the Depression-era publication of *The Grapes of Wrath* by John Steinbeck and *Factories in the Field* by Carey McWilliams. The La Follette Committee, empowered by Congress in 1936 to investi-gate allegations that American employers were denying workers their civil rights and interfering with efforts to organize unions, found damning evidence that a powerful group of California farmers had relentlessly repressed, harassed, and exploited farm labor. The 1960 airing on CBS-affiliated television stations of the Edward R. Murrow documentary "Harvest of Shame" provided starkly visual and personal testimony of the poverty, indignities, and racism suffered by farmworkers in Florida.

A few years later, a rash of violent confrontations between Cali-fornia growers and supporters of the UFW attracted intense na-tional attention and won farmworkers a fair measure of sympathy and support from urban and suburban America. This momentary notoriety no doubt helped secure the passage in 1975 of California's Agricultural Labor Relations Act (ALRA), a relatively progressive statute that guaranteed farmworkers in that state the legal right to form unions and bargain collectively. But almost as soon as the act took effect, growers launched an offensive designed to undermine its tenets and derail the UFW's momentum. By the mid-1980s, ALRA had become almost inconsequential.

Part of the farmworkers' dilemma reflects a generalized igno-rance of their situation. In most sections of the country farm-workers are unseen, unheard, and easy to forget. Writing about poverty in the midst of plenty, social critic Michael Harrington explored what he called "the other America," which is home to the unskilled, the migrants, the aged, the minorities—all those who populate an economic underworld most Americans never encounter. Inhabitants of that world tend to live isolated lives, in remote areas or neighborhoods rarely frequented by the more prosperous. Many are reluctant to leave their homes and, as a group, they have few political advocates. These are the invisible people, Harrington said, and in their neglected and forgotten state they are permeated with failure, depressed and bereft of ambition and aspirations. "As a group they are atomized. They have no face; they have no voice" (Harrington 1962:6).

In many respects, seasonal and migrant farmworkers are citizens of the world Harrington described. They come, they go, they adapt, they accept. In the fruit- and vegetable-growing regions of states such as Michigan, Ohio, Washington, Virginia, and New York, where labor-intensive crops demand armies of short-term harvest labor, workers arrive at the start of the season and depart when the job is done. They are typically housed in small camps on growers' property and only occasionally venture into town for supplies and socializing. Few residents outside these rural farm communities ever come into contact with the workers or comprehend the pattern of their lives. Farmworkers are far more visible in states such as California, Texas, and Florida, which serve as home base to thousands of migrants and sustain a corps of settled workers who take advantage of the longer local growing season. But the larger community's concern about the workers and its willingness to alleviate their dire circumstances is muted at best.

Racism and xenophobia may explain some of the indifference to the farmworkers' plight. In the late nineteenth and early twentieth centuries, California and its citizens harshly discriminated against the Chinese and Japanese laborers who worked the fields and harvested the state's bounty. Agricultural employers in the West perceived these and subsequent groups of nonwhite immigrants as genetically suited to the rigors of farm labor and the indignities of camp living (Fisher 1953:50). These days, the public's bias is expressed in more subtle ways. Migrant workers in northern states report some merchants refuse their business and some doctors refuse them treatment. Local zoning boards deny farmers' applications to erect new or expand existing labor camps and health clinics schedule calling hours that are inconvenient for migrant workers.

One of the key maxims of the labor movement holds that self-help, by forming unions and bargaining with employers, is a potent way to improve workers' collective lot. Many groups in America have dramatically raised their standards of living and working by choosing union representation. Auto workers, steel workers, electrical workers, truck drivers, and garment workers are just a sample of those whose wages and working conditions changed drastically for the better after they organized themselves into unions and negotiated labor contracts with employers. Even with the spate of wage cuts and other contract concessions that rocked the economy during the mid–1980s and unsettled long-standing bargaining relationships, union workers in the private sector still earn on average almost 40 percent more than their unorganized peers (*Daily Labor Report*, June 21, 1993).

Farmworkers have had only minimal and rarely fruitful experience with unions. Occasional attempts to unionize the farm labor force during the past hundred years have been consistently thwarted by growers and their social, political, and judicial allies. Like many of their industrial counterparts, farmers generally abhor the very notion of labor unions, asserting that they are un-American and an infringement on farmers' property rights. And like many of their industrial counterparts, farmers have brazenly used violence and sham legal tactics to repress burgeoning union sentiment among employees.

Attempts to organize farmworkers have been complicated by the heterogeneous socioeconomic character of the population. With few notable exceptions, the hired farm labor force has historically lacked the class and group consciousness that is usually a prerequisite for union activity. Migrant and seasonal farmworkers have always been an extraordinarily diverse mix of poorly paid, relatively unskilled laborers divided by ethnicity, race, and religion who periodically converge on the nation's commercial fruit, vegetable, and horticultural farms. A smaller cohort of more highly skilled full-time workers on field crop and livestock farms, and on the largest fruit, vegetable, and horticultural farms tend to identify more with farmer-employers than with their seasonal co-workers. Such distinctions tend to diminish farmworkers' interest in collective action and have discouraged most mainstream unions from mounting and sustaining organizing drives among these workers.

The chronic oversupply of farm labor has also frustrated union campaigns. Farm work is an unskilled occupation that perennially

operators and their families. This is a decrease from less than a generation ago, when farm families took care of 75 percent of the work themselves (Martin 1985:10).

For operators whose farms outgrow the family's capabilities, however, hired labor is the only available solution. In the years immediately following World War II, there were about four million hired farmworkers in the United States. Slightly more than one-third of the 6.1 million farm operators employed paid workers, although a mere 20 percent of these farms hired 90 percent of the labor. The greatest concentration of farmworkers was found on the fruit, vegetable, and nut tree farms in California. Large numbers of hired laborers were also found on livestock ranches in Nevada and Wyoming, in the delta cotton region of the South, and on truck farms in the East (Morin 1952:5–6).

Mechanization has eliminated many of the manual jobs in commodities such as cotton, field crops, and some fruits and vegetables sold for processing. The estimated number of paid farm laborers declined precipitously between 1950 and 1970, and stabilized at around 2.6 million in the 1970s (Martin 1985:9). Farmers with hundreds of acres of grain or cotton still hire full-time employees to maintain and operate capital equipment, and probably hire some seasonal employees to help with the harvest. Even dairy operators with modern milking sheds generally need a paid employee once the herd reaches about fifty cows.

The majority of paid farmworkers, however, are the migrant and seasonal workers who harvest and cultivate the fields and orchards. Changing consumer preferences for fresh market fruits and vegetables, many of which have not yet yielded to mechanization, assure continued demand for a sizable corps of hired seasonal laborers. Growers who raise labor-intensive crops such as broccoli, strawberries, raisin grapes, and apples need small armies of temporary workers at specific times of the year. Migrant and seasonal workers are found in all fifty states, with the heaviest concentrations in California, Florida, and Texas. North Carolina, New York, Michigan, Wisconsin, Ohio, Washington, Arizona, and New Jersey also provide temporary jobs for large numbers of farmworkers.

The farm labor market is notably different from other labor markets in the American economy. Forty years ago, economist Lloyd Fisher characterized the California farm labor market as "structureless" (1953:7). By that, Fisher meant the agricultural job market was distinct from its formal and organized analogue in the manufacturing sector and distinguished by several specific attributes. First, entry into the farm labor market was relatively free and easy because of the absence of unions, job rights, or honored job preferences. Second, the relationship between employers and employees was impersonal, marked by anonymity (and accompanying racist attitudes about suitability for farm work), high turnover, and the absence of a long-term commitment between boss and worker. Third, jobs could be performed by almost anyone, including unskilled workers, and there was little or no skill-based division of labor. Fourth, pay was usually parsed out on a piece-rate system, which voided the need to determine worker competence or productivity and reinforced the tendency to recruit more workers than necessary. Finally, farm jobs required minimal amounts of capital equipment and thus had flexible upper limits on the number of workers actually hired (Fisher 1953:7–8).

Although Fisher's analysis is dated and not entirely applicable to the farm labor market of the 1990s, some similarities exist. High turnover and strong demand for seasonal and migrant labor means farm jobs are relatively easy to secure, especially with the right network of family and friends or connections with a farm labor contractor or crew leader who matches workers with jobs. Among that segment of the farm labor force that comes and goes during the season and seeks new opportunities in the next, there is little need or desire to establish personal relationships with employers—feelings that are no doubt reciprocated. In addition, farm work continues to be the point of entry into American society for thousands of newly arrived immigrants who lack the job and language skills needed for other kinds of work. Piece-rate payment schemes, the preferred mode of compensation in the 1950s, are still common today. And in most labor-intensive crops, a surfeit of workers is clearly preferable to just enough.

But in certain respects, the farm labor market has evolved into a more complicated system than that depicted by Fisher. Whereas many farmers hire workers directly and almost half of all workers find jobs through friends or relatives (Mines, Gabbard, and Samardick 1992:674), farm labor contractors who serve as middlemen increasingly dominate the recruitment and supervision of migrant and seasonal workers in many regions of the country. The power and influence of the contractors is especially keen among immigrant farmworkers, who make up 90 percent of the contract crews (Mines, Gabbard, and Samardick 1992:674). As the immigrant share of the farm labor force grows, so will the control of labor contractors who have the ability to erect barriers to entry by deciding who will and will not get jobs.

Crews are usually tight-knit groups whose members are linked by familial, ethnic, and religious bonds. Job assignments typically reflect a seniority-, skill-, gender-, and age-based division of labor, with young migrant men specializing in harvest tasks and U.S.-born workers doing more of the semiskilled pre- and post-harvest tasks (Mines, Gabbard, and Samardick 1992:681). Although many farm jobs still do not require formal training or education, workers are not perfect substitutes for each other and tend to specialize by crop and task. Celery cutters, for example, are high-skill (and high-wage) workers who belong to crews that cut only celery. Technological advances, changing consumer preferences, the growth of urban markets, and the availability of rapid and reliable transportation have forced the farm labor market to adapt and assume a structure that was neither apparent nor relevant in Fisher's day.

Fisher also argued (correctly) that significant wage differentials between farm and factory would persist long into the future. In 1950, three years before Fisher's volume was published, farm wages were about 40 percent of nonfarm wages. Since the late 1970s, farm wages seem to have stabilized at slightly more than 50 percent of nonfarm wages (Commission on Agricultural Workers 1992:47), which translates to a significantly lower amount when the dollar value of industrial workers' benefits is taken into account. Migrant and seasonal farmworkers lack the traditional array of fringes such as health insurance, vacation and sick leave, retirement benefits, and disability, which increase the value of workers' wages by about 40 percent. An estimated 22 percent of all hired farmworkers receive employer-subsidized housing, but this "benefit" often comes at the price of slightly lower pay (Mines, Gabbard, and Samardick 1992:675). Wages for migrant and seasonal workers are depressed by such factors as immobility between agricultural jobs and industrial jobs, a surplus of workers in the farm labor market, the absence of strong unions, and employer organizations and informal grower groups that unilaterally set wages.

Reported farm wages for all paid farm employees unadjusted for inflation averaged $5.57 an hour in 1991 but varied significantly by region, crop, job, and method of payment (piece-rate workers earn the most when their work is translated into hourly rates). The hiring arrangement also affects pay, with workers in the direct employ of farmers earning higher hourly rates than those employed by farm labor contractors (Commission on Agricultural Workers 1992:93–97). These figures do not, however, account for employers who pay below legal minimums or bilk workers by not paying the promised rate or by deducting from their wages frivolous and illegal charges for such items as transportation to and from the fields, drinking water, liquor, or generic unexplained fees.

Depending on the commodity, wages represent between 5 percent and 28 percent of farmers' total production costs, with the national average estimated at 11.5 percent (Commission on Agricultural Workers 1992:33). The share of costs paid as wages is lowest in capital-intensive field-crop and hog and cattle farms and highest on fruit farms. Because farmers are vulnerable to the influence of food processors, retail chains, the weather and other natural occurrences, and national fiscal and political policies, wages are one of the few costs they can control. Wages loom as a variable cost that can and must be minimized.

Over the years, this realization has prompted growers of perishable crops to demand a plentiful, docile, and passive labor force. Historians and researchers have long noted that much of California's success in developing large-scale, labor-intensive agriculture is rooted in local farmers' enduring access to an oversupply of labor. Growers managed this feat through sustained importation of foreign workers, promotion of lax immigration controls, and over-recruitment of workers to individual farms. They understood all too well that an excess supply of labor would ensure low wages and miserable working conditions, and worker resignation about the situation. Militant anti-unionism and a preference for a succession of foreign workers, and racial and ethnic minority workers, was the logical outgrowth of growers' drive to control the labor market.

Curiously, on the farm itself this need for control stops well short of careful and skilled management of the labor force. Most farmers who require paid labor put only cursory effort into managing and nurturing it. Oftentimes farm employers relegate the responsibility to outside labor contractors who recruit and supervise the workers, frequently with a crude and brutal hand. Sometimes growers manage workers themselves but invest as little energy and creativity as possible. The apparent rationale is that farmers' primary concerns center around enduring assets: land, crops, capital. Labor, by contrast, is expendable: labor comes and goes.

Labor experts and academics who specialize in agriculture are aware of this bias. Few have built their careers on issues pertaining to the management and development of farm labor or to the nature of farmer-worker interactions. No one knows for sure whether more care and attention to employee-employer relations and improved working conditions will net positive returns, measured by such outcomes as productivity gains and worker retention, or will place additional and unnecessary financial and management burdens on already harried farmers. Most of the attention paid to farm labor relations was framed as economic analyses of the farm labor market or as historical and institutional discourses on the seeming inability of farmworkers to organize and sustain a flourishing union movement.

Interest in these issues seems to be growing. In the past few years, for example, a number of universities and affiliated cooperative extension services have embraced the notion of farm labor relations and either launched research projects or begun offering workshops and newsletters on farm-specific human resource management. The motivating spark may have less to do with moral indignation about farmworkers' living and working conditions than with concern about work-force quality and relatively uncontrollable market forces. That is, there is a burgeoning recognition among farmers and researchers that better training and supervision, a degree of job security, and improved working conditions may, in fact, enhance efficiency and productivity. There is also anxious awareness of the imbalance between the supply of, and demand for, farm labor. In certain parts of the country, supply is two to three times greater than demand. Unchecked immigration has swelled the farm labor population in states along the southern border of the United States, while the amnesty feature of IRCA has emboldened formerly illegal immigrants to travel far afield in search of jobs. In some regions of the Northeast, however, farm operators are experiencing spot shortages of seasonal employees and are also having trouble finding skilled and committed full-time workers.

The locus of attention in farm labor relations has long been California. The reasons are obvious. California is by far the largest user of hired agricultural labor in the country: growers there employ one-quarter of the hired farm labor in the United States. Many California farms are giant commercial enterprises that grow labor-intensive fruits, vegetables, and horticultural products. There are at least 750,000 farmworkers in the state and more than three-quarters of the state's farm work is performed by paid employees (Martin, Vaupel, and Egan 1988:xi, 2). The largest commercial operations hire thousands of employees at the height of the season and provide scores of pre- and post-harvest preparation and clean-up jobs, and a few dozen full-time jobs in maintenance, machine repair, marketing, and the like. In these and some smaller enterprises, a primitive industrial relations system with rules governing the interaction between labor and management has evolved.

California is also home to a tradition of farm labor activism that dates to the nineteenth century, when thousands of foreign workers were imported into the state to fill crucial, yet undesirable, jobs. Farm labor unions have periodically enjoyed modest success in California largely because farmworkers there have been the most consistently self-conscious and militant group of farm employees in the country. More strikes have been mounted in California than elsewhere, as have more attempts to organize farm employees (Morin 1952:15). A spate of successful, though short-lived, organizing drives occurred in the midst of the Depression. During the 1960s and 1970s, Cesar Chavez and the UFW emerged from the California fields to lead a series of triumphant organizing campaigns, negotiate a few hundred labor contracts, and posit, albeit temporarily, the cause of farmworkers on the national agenda. California farm employees have also made the greatest strides in securing legal protections denied their peers in most other states.

The Evolution of the Migrant and Seasonal Worker

For many Americans the word farmworker evokes an image of the migrant laborer who travels with the harvest, moving from farm to farm and region to region in perpetual search of a few days' work. Although many full-time farmworkers are permanently rooted in established communities, their hold on the popular imagination is considerably more tenuous. These workers have played an unheralded but pivotal role in the evolution of rural America, providing their services to farmers in need of extra help and sometimes relying on their own paid labors to prop up their failing enterprises or seed their dreams of proprietary ownership in a piece of land. For the most part, full-time farmworkers were (and are) members of the same socioeconomic class as their employers, and thus lived and worked alongside the farmer and his family. Perhaps these simple sociological facts explain some of the public disinterest in the coterie of full-time farm laborers.

The story of this country's migrant and seasonal farmworkers is only slightly more familiar. The genesis of the migrant farm labor system can be traced to California, where patterns of land owner-ship combined with economic and climatic factors to spawn a labor-intensive, high-value fruit, vegetable, and horticultural sector. It was in reference to California that the term "industrial agriculture" was coined and, with it, the image of thousands of bedraggled and hungry farmworker families roving the countryside on the lookout for yet another exploitative job. The feudal empires that are the legacies of Spanish colonial rule and the Caucasian population's fierce xenophobia and racism laid the foundation for the enduring presence of a dispossessed and occasionally militant class of farm-workers (McWilliams 1939).

Both large ranchers and government officials in California have been blamed for their symbiotic collusion in the development of top-heavy and socially irresponsible land policies that shut out settlers and led to waste and ecological neglect (McWilliams 1939:21). During the latter part of the nineteenth century, landowners de-cided that profits from raising wheat and other grains were too low. So they devised a new strategy, one based on labor-intensive crops that yielded high revenues per acre, and rearranged their opera-tions. Within a few years, fruits and vegetables and irrigation and diversification became hallmarks of the state's prodigious agri-cultural sector.

From then on, the vast farms in the fertile inland valleys and along the coast were dependent on cheap and plentiful supplies of temporary labor. Sometime around 1870, managers and owners of the great estates realized that immigration was the answer to their labor needs. Although Americans did indeed participate in the farm labor force, large landowners argued that American workers were disinterested in and unsuited for farmwork but that immi-grants would be grateful for the jobs. Equally important to the landowners was the expectation that immigrant workers were likely to quit the area once the seasonal planting and harvesting were completed, leaving the community's underlying social structure undisturbed.

The growers' preferences were accommodated: successive waves of immigrant groups have since been the mainstays of California agriculture. First came the Chinese, who were imported to work the mines and build the railroads, but who were later forced onto farms when they could find no alternative employment. By the 1890s, labor unions and small manufacturers and farmers who had no need for cheap foreign labor resented what they perceived as the large growers' unfair competitive advantage. They waged a noisy campaign that resulted in the exclusion of the Chinese from the California fields.

Within a few years, Japanese workers arrived to fill the labor gap and were regarded by farm employers as just another racial minority to be exploited. Japanese workers proved efficient and industrious, and they helped establish the local sugar beet and rice industries. They maintained strong ethnic and community ties and created clubs, or associations, that coordinated labor supply and functioned as quasi-unions. But the Japanese workers' tenure did not last long. Their strong entrepreneurial ambitions and skills, coupled with the general populace's anti-Asian sentiment during the early 1900s, once again drove immigrant workers from the fields and denied the large estates an abundant source of low-wage labor.

Meanwhile, other ethnic groups were gaining footholds in certain crops. Armenians migrated from the East Coast and gravitated to the state's raisin farms. Italian immigrants found work in the artichoke fields and vineyards, and Portuguese workers were hired into dairies. Farmers were unabashed in their attempts to control the labor force by using one ethnic group against another. Between 1907 and 1910, an influx of Hindus who worked for a pittance allowed farmers to beat down the wages offered workers belonging to other racial and ethnic communities (McWilliams 1939:117).

Immigration from Europe practically ceased during World War I and farmers looked to Mexico as a substitute source of labor. Mexicans were considered hard workers who did not complain and, best of all, returned home at the end of the season. Growers in the Southwest, who found ready allies among railroad and mining companies, convinced the U.S. Department of Labor that labor shortages required the waiver of immigration restrictions for Mexican workers (Majka and Majka 1982:62). Agricultural lobbyists fought a fierce battle against rising national sentiment for immigration quotas and succeeded in winning an exemption for Mexican farmworkers from the 1924 Immigration Act. But their good fortune did not hold and over the next few years several attempts to limit Mexican immigration prompted growers to seek some insurance. Casting about for an impregnable source of labor, California growers found their supply in an American colony, the Philippines. In the latter part of the 1920s, Filipino farmworkers began entering the state and secured jobs by accepting lower wages and crossing picket lines.

The irony in this chronicle of desperately needed immigrant farmworkers was the vicious treatment accorded them by state officials and the local population. Rampant discrimination and blatant racism expressed by farm employers and nonfarm residents alike turned farmworkers into a permanent underclass of transient and powerless people. The presence of immigrant workers in the state also pointed up the wide divergence of interests between California's landed gentry and the rest of its citizens, who were jealous and bitter about the low-wage labor available to the agricultural elite. But given California's social, political, and economic climate, it is not surprising that the needs and concerns of the large, commercial farm operators ultimately prevailed.

The Birth of Farmworker Activism

Despite the farmworkers' subservient and tenuous position in society, many immigrant and American workers actively rebelled against their situation. The 1913 Wheatland Riot, which took place on a California hops ranch and involved almost three thousand men, women, and children, was a desperate protest against inhumane housing and sanitary conditions and a collective outcry against farmers' practice of recruiting many more workers than they actually needed. The International Workers of the World (or IWW, a militant union of anarchists commonly known as the "Wobblies") had already organized about 8 percent of the migrant work force in California by that time (Moore 1965:124) and was intent on setting up agricultural locals around the state. But within a few years the Wobblies were decimated by government raids on their offices and by the arrests and trials of union leaders whom officials alleged were radical terrorists.

More strikes and riots by disgruntled American, Mexican, and Filipino farmworkers followed on and off well into the Depression years. Spontaneous and, occasionally, planned strikes broke out around the state in the early 1930s. These strikes involved thousands of farmworkers, including the more than fifteen thousand cotton workers in the San Joaquin Valley who walked out for twenty-four days in 1933 (Stein 1973:224). The Cannery and Agricultural Workers Industrial Union (CAWIU), an offshoot of the Communist-affiliated Trade Union Unity League (TUUL), played an active role in the fields for a brief time, particularly among migrant workers from Mexico. CAWIU provided organizational and tactical skills in several dozen strikes that were staged over wages and control issues, such as farm-specific worker negotiating committees and using the union rather than labor contractors to recruit employees (Majka and Majka 1982:76).

Wherever workers took an activist stance, their union sympathies were quickly and savagely contained by arrests, court injunctions, and vigilante action. Adopting tactics long familiar to industrial employers, growers colluded with leading citizens, bankers, and merchants, and with sheriffs, judges, and mayors to stage sham trials, murders, violence, firings, and Communist-baiting in a determined attempt to maintain control over the work force. CAWIU disappeared in 1935, its leaders jailed and the Communists no longer interested in supporting an alternative and ideologically based union movement. Growers reveled in the absence of labor strife and the self-congratulatory assumption that their tough response had worked.

Within a couple of years, however, a new union began organizing farmworkers. Founded in Denver in 1937, the United Canning, Agricultural, Packing and Allied Workers of America (UCAPAWA) was a national organization chartered by the fledgling Congress of Industrial Organizations (CIO) and thus formally allied to the burgeoning industrial union movement. UCAPAWA initially focused its organizing efforts on California's food processing plants but was stymied by the labor movement's internal rivalries and politics (Majka and Majka 1982:127). The union then shifted its attention to the fields, where many Mexican and Filipino migrants had been replaced by the dust bowl migrants, or Okies, who were streaming into the state in search of jobs and new homes. The labor camps run by the Farm Services Administration (FSA), which housed the new migrants and attempted to instill in them a collectivist ideal and democratic habits, were quickly identified as natural recruiting sites. UCAPAWA organizers were welcomed into a number of camps by managers who made space available for offices and meetings and provided access to the camp newspaper (Stein 1973:252).

But UCAPAWA efforts quickly fizzled. A series of wildcat strikes by fruit and vegetable workers between 1937 and 1939 were unrelated to UCAPAWA activities. Although the union did organize and lead a two-week strike by San Joaquin Valley cotton workers in 1939, the action barely affected the picking and achieved no gains for the workers. Violent and intimidating tactics by growers and their official allies no doubt helped squash UCAPAWA's bid to build a farm labor union.

The failure also reflected the Okies' indifference, if not outright hostility, to the idea and specifics of UCAPAWA membership. Union leaders were politically radical, and charges of Communist influence alienated the Okies, who were fierce in their particular brand of patriotism. Moreover, the Okies were not capable of responding to the union's entreaties. Their migration had left them demoralized, defenseless, and disoriented, and they were unable to mount the effort required to engage in collective action for the collective good. As they settled and assimilated into the local milieu, their own tradition of rugged individualism reasserted itself and merged with the larger community's anti-union attitudes. By 1940, UCAPAWA was ready to acknowledge defeat and promptly quit the fields and moved on to the canneries (Stein 1973:256–64).

California farmworkers were hardly alone in expressing their outrage during the Depression years. Labor activism among industrial workers was similarly intense, widespread, and edged with violence and ideological overtones. Among workers in the fields, small unions cropped up throughout the country in states as diverse as New Jersey, Illinois, Colorado, and Montana as workers cried out against low wages and pitiful working conditions.

Tenant farmers and sharecroppers in the Arkansas delta also began dissenting against the vestiges of a plantation economy that trapped blacks and whites alike in dire poverty and servitude. Landowners financially and physically abused the people who worked their property, and through a form of what could only be described as legalized slavery that evolved in the post-Reconstruction years, they managed to subdue and dominate an uneducated and dejected population. Greedy landlords seemed shameless and cavalierly manipulated payments, credits, and rents to their advantage. They even denied the croppers and tenants their rightful share of Depression-era programs that pulled acres out of production and were meant to provide monetary relief to producers while artificially raising the price of cotton and other cash crops (Grubbs 1971:3–10, 20–23).

Enraged by such outright theft and exploitation, two Arkansas businessmen and Socialist Party organizers, H. L. Mitchell and Clay East, launched the Southern Tenant Farmers' Union (STFU) in 1934. For several years thereafter, the STFU was a powerful voice for disposessed small farmers and sharecroppers. For a time it organized racially integrated locals, reasoning that black and white tenants and croppers were victimized by the same system and shared the same goals. Union leaders also lobbied in Washington, D.C., to generate sympathy for their members and demand reformulated policies that would close the loopholes and right the wrongs pervading local implementation of the federal Agricultural Adjustment Administration (AAA), a New Deal program designed to raise crop prices by paying farmers to take acreage out of production.

Mitchell and East were determined to make the organization a true union. Inspired by socialist ideas, they were nonetheless true pragmatists. They encouraged the development of grass-roots leaders, both black and white, and tried to reach potential constituents by playing to their values and relying on local institutions. They organized plantation by plantation, collected dues whenever and wherever they could, and occasionally mounted strikes to impress upon landlords the union's strength and viability. Mitchell and East won friends in high places—liberals, intellectuals, and political and church activists who pressed the STFU cause in Washington and helped secure funds to keep the organization alive.

But like farmworkers in other parts of the country, this group of Arkansas tenants and sharecroppers who dared demand their rights inevitably ran afoul of the local establishment. Unabashed hostility and violence by landowners and government officials met the protesters' every move. Union supporters were summarily evicted from their homes, murdered, confined on private prison farms, and tried by kangaroo courts. The establishment's fiercest enmity was reserved for black STFU members. Utilizing a socially and politically acceptable cover, the tumult was blamed on the usual band of outside agitators: northerners and Communists.

The STFU, much like the CAWIU, faded away in the early 1940s without ever realizing its goals of security and fair treatment for tenant farmers and sharecroppers. The STFU's merger (from 1937 to 1939) with UCAPAWA, the Communist-led affiliate of the CIO, sealed its eventual demise as the union was torn asunder by internecine ideological battles and fights with UCAPAWA over STFU autonomy. By 1941, the STFU had passed into the hands of racist leaders and its progressive tradition was a paean to the past.

Yet the union left its mark. The STFU succeeded in putting the issue of rural poverty on the national agenda during Roosevelt's second administration (Grubbs 1971:117). And it kept alive the idea of linking farmworkers to the mainstream labor movement. Indeed, in 1946 STFU founder Mitchell convinced the American Federation of Labor (AFL) to charter the National Farm Labor Union (NFLU), an organization that endured for fourteen years. But what is perhaps the STFU's greatest legacy is shrouded in unintended irony: many of its landless constituents formed the nucleus of a new corps of migrant farmworkers, southern blacks who trekked up and down the East Coast as the seasons changed and the crops matured.

Although the history of farmworker strikes and farm labor organizing is decades old, most unions suffered the fate of the STFU. Few unions survived more than several years or accomplished much for the workers. Details about these early campaigns remain elusive and it is difficult to draw more than superficial conclusions about the why and how of these events. Even Stuart Jamieson, the author of an exhaustive study of most known incidents of farm labor activism up through the early 1940s, conceded the precise history and character of farmworker uprisings was difficult to document (Jamieson [1945] 1976:1). What we do know, however, is that farmworkers in every region of the country have at one time or another engaged in collective action to protest their treatment by employers.

Much of the labor unrest seems to have stemmed from the socioeconomic changes that rippled through American agriculture in the first four decades of this century. The mutually reinforcing trends toward concentration of production in fewer but larger farms and crop specialization together generated intensified demand for hired farm labor. Along with the growth of large-scale farming, and the parallel diminution in the social and economic importance of traditional family farms, came the inevitable development of an industrial-style labor relations system that was marked by inequality between employers and employees, sharply delineated roles that ensured impersonal relationships between worker and boss, and employers who were motivated to seek ever higher profits while employees were relegated to the drudgery of standardized, repetitive work (Jamieson [1945] 1976:2–8).

The byproduct of this dynamic was labor activism. Sometimes the disaffection was manifest as a formal union and sometimes as a spontaneous outbreak by groups of workers aggrieved about various issues. The amount of labor unrest varied by region and was typically crop specific. Unions and ad hoc groups usually revolved around indigenous leaders and these organizations frequently dissolved once their grievances were addressed or their actions repressed by hostile employers and local governmental authorities. The height of farmworker activism occurred during the Depression, when farm prices and wages were at their lowest and the supply of farm labor was swollen by the massive migration of displaced dust bowl families.

The Bracero and Other Contract Labor Programs

The Depression was soon overtaken by World War II and thousands of farmworkers were absorbed into wartime industrial production. By the early 1940s, farmers perceived that they were facing yet another labor-related challenge. In place of the labor activism that had enraged and threatened so many farmers just a few years earlier, commercial farmers in the Southwest and on the West Coast began complaining about war-induced labor shortages. Their cries were heard by the Roosevelt administration, which in 1942 reached agreement with the Mexican government for the legal importation of temporary workers, or braceros, for American farms. During the next twenty-two years, until the bracero program was finally phased out in 1964, more than four million Mexican farmworkers legally contracted to work on U.S. farms. At its peak in

1956, the bracero program supplied 445,000 Mexican workers to American farmers and constituted one-third of the seasonal agricultural work force in California (Commission on Agricultural Workers 1992:17, 18).

Stark self-interest seems to have motivated farmers' pursuit of the braceros. Mexican workers had been fixtures of the California farm labor force since the 1920s and were known to be hardworking and malleable. Despite the Mexican workers' support for many Depression-era strikes, growers considered them desirable employees, usually preferring Mexicans over available domestic workers. Growers regarded the bracero program as a way to tighten their control over the farm labor force and to solidify its migrant character (Majka and Majka 1982:136).

The growers achieved their goals. The federally sponsored bracero program satisfied peak labor needs and also undermined attempts to permanently settle migrant and seasonal farmworkers, sabotaged union organizing activities, froze farm wages at rock-bottom levels, and provided labor-related subsidies to large-scale growers (Majka and Majka 1982:140–42). When the Korean War began, the agricultural community once again raised the spectre of labor shortages and, in 1951, convinced Congress to enact Public Law 78, which put the bracero program on more permanent footing by creating an administrative framework for recruiting, contracting, and transporting braceros to American firms.

By the 1960s, however, perceptions of the program had begun to change. The public became increasingly concerned about abusive treatment of the braceros and the program's negative impact on domestic farmworkers. Even some growers began grumbling about the amount of regulation and paperwork involved with the braceros. Indeed, changing cultural and political mores forced a re-evaluation of the system. In 1964, a powerful alliance of liberals, labor unions, and church and civic associations framed the issue against the nation's budding interest in civil rights and finally convinced a Congress already concerned about lax administration and corruption in the bracero program not to renew Public Law 78.

By that time, however, immigrant Mexican farmworkers had become a permanent feature of the nation's labor force. Many former braceros had legally settled in California and Texas, and they continued working in agriculture. Although Congress stayed the legal importation of temporary field workers through the bracero program, thousands of Mexican workers nonetheless poured into the United States and firmly entrenched the nation's dependence on an immigrant and often illegal agricultural work force.

A system of foreign contract labor similar to the bracero program cropped up on the East Coast as well. Not to be outdone by their vocal and determined western colleagues, eastern farmers also convinced the federal government that a war-induced labor shortage demanded action. In 1943, the United States signed agreements with several Caribbean islands that inaugurated an annual back-and-forth migration that continues to this day.

The Emergence of the United Farm Workers

The appearance of the charismatic Cesar Chavez and the UFW in the mid-1960s marked another turning point in farmworker history. Chavez and his California-based union galvanized many of the state's farmworkers and eventually won the sympathy and support of a large portion of the American population. For the few years that the union aggressively fought for recognition and won labor contracts for its members, the UFW was able to tangibly improve farmworkers' lives. But even more importantly, it helped win for members and nonmembers alike the dignity and self-respect that had long eluded them.

The central theme behind the UFW's crusade was the debilitating effect on workers of the growers' determined cultivation of labor surpluses and their failure to develop self-policing measures that would prevent outright exploitation. The combination of too many workers and too much abuse had long fueled occasional dissent and rebellion. Strikes against large ranches broke out after World War II, and resentment toward the braceros, who were often used as strike-breakers, began to blossom in the late 1950s. But like most of the earlier agricultural strikes, these uprisings were also doomed to failure. The almost unlimited availability of workers willing to cross picket lines, the strike-related loss of income by people with few alternative resources, and the unrelenting efforts by employers to repress strike activity made work stoppages a dubious weapon.

One way to understand farmworker insurgency in the post-World War II years is to divide the era into three distinct periods (Jenkins and Perrow 1977:254). The first activist phase lasted from 1947 to

1955 and was led by the NFLU, which adopted an industrial model of organizing that stressed enrolling members who worked on the large California farms and then initiating strikes over wages and working conditions. The union also tried calling attention to the negative impact of the braceros, whose presence depressed wages and enabled growers to break strikes with impunity. In the end, the NFLU failed to attract much support from California's farmworkers or anyone else.

The second phase encompassed the years between 1956 and 1964, when the Agricultural Workers Organizing Committee (AWOC) mounted sporadic organizing campaigns. Created by the AFL-CIO in 1959 at the behest of Walter Reuther, then president of the UAW, AWOC embraced an organizing model that was unsuited for farm laborers. AWOC conceived its mission in terms of what the leadership knew best: private sector manufacturing. Its staff knew little about farm labor. They sought out members from among the dust bowl and other Anglo migrant communities and tried to organize farm labor contractors, much the way craft unions in the AFL-CIO organized construction industry contractors. Like the NFLU, AWOC harped on economic goals and never built a base of support among its constituents or in the larger society. This was also a time when changing political alignments led to the emergence of a reform coalition, which proved crucial to the farmworkers during the next decade (Jenkins and Perrow 1977:259–62).

The last period began in the mid-1960s with the emergence of the United Farm Workers Organizing Committee (UFWOC) under the direction of Chavez. The confluence of social, political, and economic factors that sustained and supported the farmworker movement and propelled it toward success distinguishes this third period from the earlier two (Jenkins and Perrow 1977:266).

The mid-1960s was one of those occasional historical moments when shifts in the political and social landscape provided marginal and excluded groups an opportunity to advance their interests. Congress killed the bracero program in 1964, as the country first awakened to the civil rights movement. Students began to assert their claims, and the anti-war movement was about to be born. In this increasingly progressive and tolerant environment, California's farmworkers finally began to score some victories.

Engaging in highly visible collective action, Chavez and a fiercely dedicated group of followers made masterful use of what sociologists call the "resource mobilization theory," an explanation of social change that focuses on transformations in the structure of economic and political power (Jenkins 1985:1). Chavez took full advantage of the highly charged political atmosphere of the 1960s. He rallied to the farmworkers' cause the critical support of liberals, social and religious activists, politicians, students, labor leaders, and mainstream union members. Although thousands of farmworkers played key roles in the fervent struggle for recognition and better lives, the energy, commitment, status, and money of these nonfarm outsiders was critical to the UFW's success (Jenkins and Perrow 1977:251). No other farmworker movements had intersected so completely with the larger society or been blessed with such a ripe and welcoming political environment, and no other farm union ever accomplished what the UFW managed to do.

Chavez, who died in April 1993, was a former farmworker and committed community organizer who decided in late 1961 to break with the Community Service Organization (CSO) and its urban civil rights focus in order to devote his energies to organizing Mexican-American farmworkers. Chavez learned invaluable lessons from veteran organizers Saul Alinsky and Fred Ross during the ten years he worked with the CSO, and proved to be gifted at his calling. From his mentors Chavez borrowed and adapted strategies and tactics that stressed nonviolence, building a sense of community, teaching people the rights and responsibilities of citizenship, defining and understanding workers' issues, and creating service programs that would meet critical community needs.

Several months after leaving the CSO, Chavez founded the Farm Workers Association (FWA) and set up shop in Delano, the heart of the grape-growing region of the southern San Joaquin Valley. Chavez recognized the futility of organizing a union without first organizing a base of support built around the farmworkers' needs. Together with a small group of associates, Chavez held house meetings, talked to people on the streets and in cafes, set up a credit union and auto parts co-op, and offered burial insurance. The group's activities began attracting attention and in 1965 it formed an alliance with the National Migrant Ministry, an arm of the National Council of Churches.

A critical strike against Delano grape growers in the fall of 1965 brought notoriety and credibility to Chavez and the renamed National Farm Workers Association (NFWA). It raised public awareness of the farmworkers' situation and garnered crucial outside support from clergy, politicians, liberal activists, students, and labor leaders. Reuther, of the UAW, arrived in Delano in December of that year with a $10,000 contribution and the promise of $5,000 more each month.

The Delano strike was initiated by a few tight-knit crews of Filipino workers who belonged to AWOC and were led by Larry Itliong, an effective Filipino organizer. Angered by the low wages growers were offering, the workers decided to stage a sit-down in the labor camps where they lived. Chavez was initially reluctant to join the strike, fearing the movement was not yet strong enough to sustain a work stoppage. Many of his own NFWA members were decidedly more eager, however, and within days the union voted to join the Filipino workers associated with AWOC. Workers quickly launched strikes at nearby ranches and growers responded in their usual fashion, with harassment, intimidation, violence, court injunctions, and strike-breaking harvest crews. The farmworkers held out and the Delano strike continued for months, punctuated by a twenty-five-day march in the spring of 1966 to the state capital at Sacramento. Although the farmworkers did not achieve their goal, one notable outcome of the Delano era was the debut of what ultimately became the farmworkers' most potent weapon: the boycott.

About two months into the flagging strike, Chavez hit upon the idea of a product embargo. The minute several union members from Delano and student supporters from nearby Berkeley convinced members of the International Longshoremen and Warehousemen's Union (ILWU) not to load a cargo of grapes on the Oakland docks, the potential power of the boycott was clear. Thus began a series of potent consumer actions against wine and table grapes, head lettuce, brand names affiliated with recalcitrant growers, and retailers who carried the offending products. Brands such as Cutty Sark liquors, S&W canned goods, Tribuno vermouth, and Chiquita bananas were boycott targets, as were Safeway supermarkets. Over the course of the many boycotts, millions of Americans shunned the targeted goods.

Intense public scrutiny and press coverage, as well as the financial pressure of declining sales, eventually forced a number of growers to surrender. Schenley Industries, which owned thousands of acres of vineyards and produced well-known lines of wine and liquor, was the first to realize it could stop the negative publicity and restore order to its operations by recognizing the NFWA and negotiating a labor agreement. The contract Schenley signed in April 1966 increased wages by 35 cents an hour to $1.75, set up a seniority system for workers and a hiring hall that gave the union control over who would work in Schenley fields, and provided for union stewards and consultation over potentially dangerous changes in work procedures (Majka and Majka 1982:179).

The following year, the threat of a product boycott netted Chavez recognition and contracts with wine makers Gallo, Almaden, Paul Masson, Christian Brothers, and Franzia. A group of grape growers in Coachella signed contracts with Chavez in the spring of 1970 and Delano growers signed on that summer. The farmworkers now had 85 percent of the California table grape industry under contract. Within three years, Chavez could boast 180 contracts covering 40,000 jobs and almost 70,000 members (Martin, Vaupel, and Egan 1988:35).

In the midst of the farmworkers' struggle with growers, the Western Conference of Teamsters began flexing its muscle in the fields. The Teamsters already had a farm contract dating to 1961 with Bud Antle, one of the largest Salinas-area lettuce growers. The reasons for Antle's link with the Teamsters remain obscure; the connection may have represented a preemptive move to ward off AWOC picketing against the braceros Antle was hiring at the time (Meister and Loftis 1977:102) or a much-needed cash infusion from the financially strong union (Friedland, Barton, and Thomas 1981:79). Five years later, the Teamsters resurfaced at vineyards owned by the DiGiorgio Corporation, a prime target of NFWA strike and boycott activities. The giant conglomerate hid behind an array of legal maneuvers, bogus negotiations, rigged elections, and all the while colluded with the Teamsters to repulse Chavez and his union. The tactics eventually worked: although the farmworkers won an election in 1966 and eventually negotiated a contract, within two years DiGiorgio had sold off its land and the new owners refused to recognize Chavez's union.

The exact motive for the Teamsters' subsequent foray into the farm labor arena remains ambiguous. No shortage of hypotheses abound. For example, the move may have reflected internal rivalries over matters of turf and power. Perhaps it was an attempt to protect the Teamsters' jurisdictional control over cannery and packing shed workers from encroachment by the farmworkers. Maybe the Teamsters were determined to protect those members whose livelihoods were negatively affected by the ongoing wave of strikes and ever-strengthening boycotts. The Teamsters' interest in the farmworkers may also have been piqued by its distaste for the NFWA's militant, grass-roots style and an expectation that growers would readily accept the Teamsters as an effective foil to Chavez (Majka and Majka 1982:180).

The Teamsters proved to be vicious foes indeed. Because they were perceived as allies of the growers, the Teamsters often won the sympathies of local sheriffs and police officers who arrested and sometimes beat Chavez's supporters. They hired thugs and strike-breakers who carried on a campaign of violence and intimidation. For their efforts, the Teamsters earned sweetheart contracts with hundreds of fruit and vegetable growers in the Salinas, Coachella, Santa Maria, and San Joaquin valleys. Many contracts were snatched from Chavez's union as soon as the opportunity arose.

By the end of 1973, the Teamsters' agricultural portfolio had swollen to 305 contracts covering 35,000 fieldworkers and the UFW's had plummeted to 14 agreements covering 6,500 workers (Martin, Vaupel, and Egan 1988:35). Most of the Teamsters' pacts, however, were sham documents. Recognition from growers and signed contracts were typically bilateral agreements between growers and union leaders, with no input from farmworkers themselves. There were few or no efforts to hold representation elections or to ratify the contract through democratic procedures. Many pacts were signed even before details were worked out. While the wage settlements generally improved on the status quo, there were no provisions allowing workers to press grievances against employers through union representatives or protections against pesticide use and continued hiring through unsavory labor contractors (Meister and Loftis 1977:167).

Chavez recognized the danger posed by the Teamsters but lacked the power to contain it. In 1967, under the aegis of several activist priests, Chavez and the Teamsters negotiated the first of a series of turf agreements that would span the next seventeen years. These arrangements ostensibly left field organizing to the NFWA, and packinghouse workers, who were covered by the NLRA, were left to the Teamsters. But most of the agreements did not hold and the Teamsters' assault, coupled with bitter repression by local authorities and grower vigilantism, soon took its toll on the farmworkers' union. The bitter rivalry continued until the 1980s, when both organizations' energy for the fight waned sharply.

After several years of frustrating strikes, boycotts, court-imposed injunctions, and unremitting pressure from the Teamsters, Chavez decided the NFWA needed a larger base and more contacts with mainstream labor. Leaders at the AFL-CIO, meanwhile, had lost faith in its AWOC affiliate and were impressed by the unexpected tenacity and strength of the NFWA. The two farmworker organizations merged in August 1967 and the United Farm Workers Organizing Committee (UFWOC) was born. Itliong, who helped instigate the Delano strike, assumed a leadership role in the new organization along with another fiery and committed lieutenant, Dolores Huerta. UFWOC retained AWOC's affiliation with the AFL-CIO and officially became the United Farm Workers of America (UFW) in 1972.

Apart from the political, financial, and moral support the NFWA/UFW received from outside supporters, a key factor in the union's relative success was its creative organizing strategy. During the union's heyday in the 1960s and early 1970s, Chavez devised and implemented tactics that were perfectly suited to the population he wanted to reach. He focused initially on the relatively stable, settled farmworkers who were more accessible and secure than their migrant coworkers. He used the community's dominant Mexican and Catholic heritage as a rallying point for activities aimed at building group solidarity. The NFWA, and later UFWOC, sponsored festivals, house meetings, and parades that sparked dedication to the community as well as to Chavez's organization. Chavez tried to engender a feeling of sacrifice and commitment among the workers and established structures of mutual aid and assistance that gave people a reason to join his movement. Only when he had built a solid base of support did Chavez inject into his organizing campaigns such traditional union concerns as wages and working conditions.

In time, Chavez became like a god to many farmworkers and political liberals. He carefully built on his constituents' shared ethnic, religious, and cultural identity, and he successfully appealed to the general population's sense of justice and fair play. He stressed the moral superiority of nonviolent actions in the face of shockingly brutal offensives by growers and their deputies. Chavez undertook a number of penitential fasts that helped draw attention to, and evoke sympathy for, the farmworkers' cause. The issues Chavez raised, including field sanitation, use of dangerous pesticides, and workers' survival needs, attracted wide public attention and backing from articulate and politically involved Americans. And the consumer boycott provided a vehicle for nonfarm sympathizers to participate in the struggle.

Farmworker activism escalated in the early 1970s. The era was marked by more violent strikes, pitched battles between the Teamsters and UFW supporters, and continued boycott pressure. The growers' repressive and judicial counterattacks against the farmworkers were having little effect, and the mayhem and negative publicity finally began gnawing at them. Attempts in the late 1960s to reform federal labor law by bringing farmworkers under the NLRA umbrella had foundered, in part because Chavez considered the law and its Taft-Hartley amendments too restrictive for a union movement in its infancy. During the early 1970s in California, several legislative efforts that would have established some kind of mechanism for mediating the conflict between growers and farmworkers also failed.

The political environment shifted dramatically with the 1974 election of Democrat Edmund G. Brown, Jr., as governor, and with a legislature controlled by the Democrats. Brown had made farmworker rights a centerpiece of his campaign. In the spring of 1975, he pulled together a group of farmers, UFW and Teamsters leaders, and politicians to work out the structure and details of a bill that would grant farmworkers the right to form unions and bargain collectively and would establish a mechanism for implementing and enforcing that right. The Agricultural Labor Relations Act (ALRA) was passed in June 1975 and took effect at the end of August.

On the surface, the state's response to the farm labor crisis seems contradictory. The centrality of agriculture to the local economy and the concomitant power wielded by agribusiness and its allies had long made state officials unquestioning supporters and promoters of agriculture. State policy on such issues as water and land use rights, and grading and packaging standards, seemed to favor the larger producers. These same growers had expressed their hostility toward the notion of farm labor unions, which promised to deny employers the dominance and control over the work force they considered their inherent right.

But the enactment of ALRA may have been less incongruous than it seems. To a large extent, the act was intended to restore order to an industry that had been periodically wracked by disruptive and often violent upheaval, especially during the previous ten years. ALRA supporters assumed such a law would bring structure, equity, and justice to a labor market that had been marred by chaos, instability, and exploitation. Indeed, the act initially attracted broad support from an array of special interests, including farm employers, farmworkers, organized labor, public advocates, lobbyists, and politicians.

ALRA seemed to satisfy a variety of needs. The act enabled state authorities to suppress and co-opt farmworker dissent through a set of modest reforms (Majka and Majka 1982:233). Farmworkers expected that ALRA would provide dignity, protection, and collective leverage in their dealings with growers while helping to improve the conditions of their lives. With few other alternatives to end the tumult and discord, growers presumed the act would spell out the rules governing farm labor relations and would peacefully entice workers back into the fields. They also figured the price was relatively cheap. Many assumed the UFW would be overpowered by the Teamsters or rebuffed by the workers, and in time would wither away. To a certain extent, they were blinded by a naive paternalism that presumed "their" workers would never reject them in favor of a union.

Passage of ALRA marked the end of an era for California agriculture. It was the culmination of years of instability and disruption in the fields, determined organizing by the UFW and its antecedents, and a debilitating rivalry between Chavez's union and the Teamsters. ALRA was hailed by many proponents and observers as a symbol of the state's progressivism. Certainly no other legislative body, at the state or federal level, had ever enacted a labor relations statute that seemed so liberal in content or tone. And certainly few other governmental units had ever done so much to protect the rights of such an economically and politically marginal group of people.

Initially, the Agricultural Labor Relations Board (ALRB), the agency established by the new law to administer and implement its provisions, was overwhelmed by demands for its services. During the first five months of the board's life, it conducted 423 union representation elections involving almost fifty thousand workers and received close to one thousand unfair labor practice complaints (ALRB

1976–77:10, 13). The fierce UFW-Teamster rivalry fueled the early election frenzy, with the UFW winning most of the elections at farms where there was no incumbent union and the Teamsters faring best where they were party to a pre-existing contract.

The ALRB caseload was so unexpectedly heavy that the initial $1.3 million appropriation was consumed within months, forcing the board to request an emergency loan from the state. Some stopgap funds were released but were insufficient to keep the board in business. In February 1976, the board shut down most of its operations and laid off the bulk of its staff. Two months later it ceased operations entirely. Objections to the act, its implementation, and the board staff were already rife in the grower community and had quickly surfaced in the legislature. Much political wrangling and an agreement between the Assembly and Senate to create a joint oversight committee finally ensured renewed and enhanced state funding. The board was back in business by July and reactivated the election process in December.

The farm union movement and the ALRB never regained momentum after the 1976 hiatus. The UFW placed a referendum on the November 1976 ballot that would have replaced ALRA with a new act containing several pro-labor provisions; it lost by a wide margin. The reconstituted board held only 188 elections in the remainder of its 1976–77 fiscal year and 122 in the following year. The trend has been downhill ever since.

Clearly, the 1970s represented the golden age for the farm union movement. By the early 1980s its energy, drive, and focus had dissipated. Organizing campaigns trailed off and the board was sponsoring no more than several dozen representation votes a year, including a sizable proportion of decertification elections (Wells and West 1989:14). Political and social changes, intense grower resistance to the act, problems internal to the UFW, and unceasing immigration of legal and illegal workers were the primary factors behind the movement's reversal of fortunes.

Whither the Farm Union Movement?

With hindsight, it seems obvious that enactment of a law protecting, and arguably facilitating, farm union organizing and collective bargaining is not sufficient to ensure that farm labor unions will flourish or that the farmworkers' standard of living and working will improve. Nonetheless, the potential for a viable farm labor movement has caused consternation in many quarters over the years.

In the period following World War II, mechanization eliminated some of the dreariest manual chores and revolutionized the agricultural sector. The assumption among many farm consultants, growers, and researchers was that the surviving corps of laborers would be a critical component of farm viability. The specter of farm labor unions caused many to wonder about the expected interplay between unions and a group of workers holding economically strategic positions.

But if farmers and agricultural labor experts were concerned about the possibility of union-led strikes and other work actions, their fears were overblown. The classic preconditions for successful union organizing seem to be missing in agriculture. Farmworkers, for example, are scattered about the countryside and are not easily accessible to each other or to union organizers. They are a diverse population in terms of class, ethnicity, race, and skill, and lack a clear community of interest. There is little employment stability in farm work, especially when jobs are threatened by machines and other workers whose skills are similar and whose wage demands are lower. The chronic oversupply of labor and the parallel ability of employers to exploit racial and national differences also undermine the ability of farmworkers to build strong unions.

Although farmworkers are among the most oppressed occupational groups in the United States, their interest in self-help through collective action has been limited. Migrant farmworkers in particular live in a comparatively unstable and erratic world marked by transience, spells of unemployment, harsh working conditions, poverty-level incomes, isolation, and deplorable living conditions. They tend to be more concerned with satisfying their immediate needs than with focusing on longer range group goals (Nelkin 1970:39). Instead of railing against the system and undertaking coordinated actions that might improve their situation, farmworkers have generally accepted the status quo and defused and mitigated their dissatisfaction by moving from job to job (Morin 1952:54). Many farmworkers, at least in years past, viewed their field worker status as temporary, an attitude that tends to dampen enthusiasm for unions and the long-term benefits to be derived from such group affiliation. And many hold negative stereotypes about unions: immigrant workers have regarded them suspiciously as "Anglo" organizations, and the Communist affiliations of such unions as CAWIU and UCAPAWA were initially hard to overcome. Grass-roots leaders who could rouse and inspire the farmworkers have also been rare.

Moreover, mainstream labor has exhibited only muted interest in farmworker organizing. The logistics of establishing units among widely dispersed and itinerant farmworkers has always seemed daunting, and generating enough dues from poorly paid workers to sustain union administrative and service obligations has been a dubious proposition. During the few instances when established labor organizations expressed interest in farmworkers, they seemed to be pursuing hidden agendas, such as protecting the jobs of members in allied occupations or trying to impede the growth of a rival union (Morin 1952:76). Even now, leaders of the AFL-CIO express interest in organizing farmworkers but have not undertaken any extraordinary efforts toward that end. There are already two farm labor unions associated with the labor federation—the UFW and the Farm Labor Organizing Committee (FLOC), which has contracts covering six thousand cucumber and tomato workers in northwestern Ohio and southeastern Michigan—and affiliated unions are typically reluctant to become embroiled in jurisdictional disputes.

Farm union activity and chances for success have also been repressed and minimized by farmers' hostility toward the notion of farm labor unions. Many farm employers believed unions would ruin what they self-righteously regarded as their close, personal relationship with employees. They argued that crop perishability made strikes potentially lethal to the enterprise and that unions represented an assault on their property and entrepreneurial prerogatives. When Communists became identified with farm labor organizing immediately before and during the Depression, the party provided farm operators a convenient foil for anti-union sentiments: it shifted the focus away from workers' legitimate grievances over wages and working conditions and placed it squarely on the alleged Communist menace.

Many of the arguments advanced by farmers to denounce unions were wrongly conceived and blatantly self-serving. Although farmers worked hard to prevent their employees from gaining leverage through collective action, for example, they themselves formed associations and cooperatives to protect and enhance their position relative to labor, lawmakers, regulators, and consumers. Several associations sprang up in California during the 1920s and 1930s: the Agricultural Labor Bureau for the purpose of recruiting and allocating labor to work the cotton and fruit crops in the San Joaquin Valley; the Associated Farmers of California to resist the Communist-inspired strikes and discord of the Depression years; and the Agricultural Producers Labor Committee whose legislative and lobbying activities were directed toward ensuring agriculture's exclusion from protective labor legislation (Fuller 1991:65–66). Farmers often acted in concert, through their organizations, to unilaterally set wages and control the supply of labor. When labor shortages developed during World War II, farmers' groups on both coasts worked with the federal government to arrange the importation of foreign workers from Canada, Mexico, the Caribbean, and Puerto Rico.

Growers exaggerated the perceived evils of work force unionization as well. They conveniently ignored the anonymous, impersonal relationships that characterized the interactions between employer and employee that prevailed on farms with hundreds of part-time workers. They overlooked the ability of other seasonal industries and those with perishable commodities to accept the potential and reality of dealing with unionized employees. They disregarded the presence of unions in factories that were family-run enterprises much like their own. In short, they refused to accept the premise advanced by the NLRA that denying workers' fundamental right to organize and bargain collectively was undemocratic and led to dislocations that disrupted commerce.

Certainly, unions in and of themselves do not guarantee that farmworkers will become better off. In his writings about this issue forty years ago, economist Lloyd Fisher was not optimistic about the future of farm labor unions. He did suggest, however, that farmworkers' lot might be improved through tighter enforcement of child labor laws, year-round jobs based on crop diversification and related nonfarm employment, prohibitions against excess worker recruitment, and regulation of labor contractors. Fisher was also a firm believer in technology and argued that fundamental gains for the workers ultimately depended on mechanization, a smaller supply of labor, and training programs for industrial jobs.

A few of these antidotes, as well as others, have been adopted; some have had a salutary effect on farmworkers' lives. Stricter child labor laws and closer scrutiny of farm labor contractors have mitigated some of the worst abuses, and machinery has replaced many of the bleakest jobs. But work for migrant and seasonal labor is still intermittent, earnings still inadequate, housing still dilapidated, respect and dignity still a rarity. Perhaps most important, the supply of labor is still far greater than the demand for labor. And on the matter of farm labor unions, the expectations of Fisher, Morin, and others have unfortunately been all too prescient.

Perhaps the 1990s will be a time when we can put to rest the argument that farmworkers cannot be organized. Potential changes in state and federal labor laws, stirrings of farmworker activism in isolated pockets of the farm sector, a growing national concern about immigration, and the labor movement's need for creative organizing strategies and outreach to low-wage immigrant and urban workers may all converge to effect a turnaround in the fortunes of farmworker unions. There are many "ifs" and "maybes" in that vision, but it is still a vision worth fighting for.

3. The Status of Farmworker Organizing

Farms and farmworkers are sprinkled throughout the United States. Relatively small, independent dairy farms predominate in certain regions of the Northeast and the Great Lakes states. Family-owned and -operated fruit and vegetable farms are found up and down the East Coast, and throughout the Midwest and California. Enormous grain and livestock operations abound in the Plains states and the Southwest. Large, specialized commercial operations that produce hundreds of thousands of dollars worth of citrus, grapes, lettuce, or tomatoes, or any of a number of row crops set the pace for the farm sector in Florida and California.

Agriculture in all of these areas is both unique and familiar. Each locale has its own customs, history, and industry structure. They also all have their share of hired workers. Some are skilled, full-time employees who are well integrated into the life of the community, while others are seasonal and transient employees who are regarded with a certain amount of hostility because of their contradictory status as much-needed outsiders. Whatever protests have arisen from among these farmworkers have been expressed by the migrant and seasonal workers, the people whose experience has been most dire.

California Update

When the California legislature enacted ALRA in 1975, its supporters predicted a sea change in farmworkers' lives. ALRA, after all, was a model piece of labor legislation. The statute did more than guarantee farmworkers the long overdue right to form unions and bargain collectively: it also embraced concepts high on the agenda of labor law reformers, such as expedited elections, and contained provisions suited to the peculiarities of agriculture. ALRA was not the first farm-specific labor law in the country— Arizona, Idaho, and Kansas enacted such legislation several years earlier—but it was certainly the most progressive in its treatment of workers and their unions.

The assumptions underlying supporters' high expectations for the act paralleled those that have long motivated union campaigns among industrial workers. Theory suggests, and practice has proven, that union representation gives voice to workers' dreams and posits power behind their words. Banding together and pressing collective goals seems to provide the leverage needed to offset, or counter-balance, the innate advantages accruing to employers who possess and control the means of production. Once confronted by a union, employers lose the ability to pit worker against worker or exploit with impunity workers' irrefutable need to earn a living. The U.S. Supreme Court long ago recognized that necessity forces employees to organize and that people need wages to support themselves and their families, but that as individuals they are incapable of resisting arbitrary and unfair treatment. Unions, the Court said in its 1921 *American Steel Foundries v. Tri-City Central Trades Council* decision, provide employees the opportunity to "deal on an equality with their employer." Sixteen years later, the Court stated that workers' fundamental right to organize and select representatives is "as clear a right" as that of employers to organize a business and select officers (*NLRB v. Jones & Laughlin Steel Corp.* [1937]).

It is easy to understand why thousands of farmworkers in the fields of California were interested in joining a union. Long regarded as chaff to be discarded when their usefulness ended, farmworkers wanted to be treated with dignity. Forced to survive on sporadic jobs and measly earnings, farmworkers wanted enough money to adequately feed and house their families. Exposed to pesticides and polluted drinking water, farmworkers wanted to live and work in safe and sanitary surroundings. Subjected to abusive treatment and sometimes outright theft, farmworkers wanted protection against unscrupulous and malicious bosses. Denied health insurance, pensions, vacations, and seniority, farmworkers wanted the basic fringe benefits possessed by nonfarm workers. Endangered for expressing dissident opinions, farmworkers wanted assurance that they could speak their minds without fear of losing their jobs or their lives.

For a short time before and after ALRA was passed, circumstances did improve for thousands of California farmworkers. As union strength grew in the decade between 1964 and 1973, farm wages jumped 120 percent and the gap between agricultural and industrial wages narrowed to 45 percent from 62 percent (Majka and Majka 1982:241). A group of vegetable growers in the Salinas area raised the ninety-cent hourly rate to almost two dollars for several thousand workers after negotiating and signing a labor contract with the UFW in 1975. In short, unionized farmworkers generally earned higher wages than unorganized workers.

Moreover, medical benefits, health and safety committees, and seniority and grievance provisions were common features of collectively bargained agreements. The farm union movement in California also helped eliminate short-handled hoes from the fields, helped secure unemployment insurance for farmworkers in that state, and raised awareness about pesticides throughout the country. But apart from the tangible progress, farmworkers also discovered the heady effects of sitting across a table and bargaining with employers as equals. Finally, farmworkers felt they had acquired dignity and respect.

Such breakthroughs, however impressive, benefited only a select group of farmworkers. Most of the union activity attaching to the UFW and the Teamsters occurred in areas with heavy concentrations of relatively stable, settled farmworkers. Workers who specialized in grapes, citrus fruits, and row crops throughout the Salinas and Ventura coastal areas and in the Imperial and San Joaquin valleys were the principal targets and beneficiaries of the union movement. A type of halo effect often extended to workers on nearby nonunion farms, as growers scrambled to stave off a union siege by raising wages and providing comparable benefits. Although no more than about 10 percent of the state's farmworkers were ever covered by union contracts, several thousand more benefited from the presence and activities of the UFW and Teamsters (Wells and West 1989:31).

Farmworkers quickly discovered the ephemeral nature of these gains. Within a few years, hourly rates began to fall and health, pension, and vacation benefits all but disappeared. California farm labor experts assert that real wages declined approximately 10 percent during the 1980s. General living and working conditions have also deteriorated. It is now not unusual to find migrant workers living in caves or fields, under trees in summer and plastic tents in winter, while others are crowded into rundown apartments, garages, and sheds in town.

The reasons for this regression are legion. Grower resistance to, and evasion of, ALRA, the proliferation of farm labor contractors, the continuing influx of legal and illegal immigrants, and the waning influence of the UFW all undermined the achievements realized by workers and their unions in the 1970s. ALRA has become increasingly irrelevant and the anticipated maturation in farm labor relations and improvements in workers' lives has yet to be realized.

Grower disenchantment with ALRA set in soon after its enactment. Zealous foes of farm labor unions, practitioners of what writers Carey McWilliams and John Steinbeck and Wisconsin senator Robert M. La Follette, Jr., called "farm fascism," growers quickly decided their initial support of the act had been misguided. Contrary to their expectations, growers were losing representation elections: during the first six months that ALRA was in effect, the ALRB conducted more than 400 elections, resulting in union wins at 84 percent of the sites (ALRB 1976–77:77–78). Growers fared just as poorly during the agency's second incarnation following the unscheduled six-month hiatus in 1976. ALRB records show 188 elections during the 1976–77 fiscal year, with union wins recorded at 89 percent of the sites. The vast majority of these victories, however, were claimed by the Christian Labor Association, a church-related group that represented workers and owners at dozens of small dairies in the San Diego area. The Western Conference of Teamsters did not participate in elections during this period because of the turf agreement signed with the UFW in March 1977.

Growers' disillusionment with the new statute intensified as they watched the ALRB in action. The trouble began with the selection of key personnel. Despite Governor Brown's earlier vow to appoint neutrals to the five-member labor board, he chose members who were regarded as liberals or were closely identified with the UFW. Growers also perceived some of the agency's professional staff to be UFW partisans, a judgment seemingly validated by evidence that included off-hours socializing between union leaders and ALRB associates.

The board's own actions further impaired its authority with growers. The general counsel's office dismissed few union complaints against growers and ALRB rulings seemed to disproportionately favor employees and/or the UFW. One of the earliest and still most controversial regulations issued by the board concerned access, or a union's right to approach workers on growers' property. In August 1975 the ALRB announced a blanket access rule that gave unions leeway in seeking out and addressing workers. The rule was based on decisions issued by the NLRB and the courts that allowed similar entrée at remote work sites where other forms of communication are ineffective (ALRB 1976–77:10). Growers were outraged and fought the ruling all the way to the U.S. Supreme Court, which declined to hear the case.

The net result of such perceived slights and pro-union bias was the withdrawal of growers' support, however grudging it had been, for ALRA and the board. Instead of seeking outright repeal of the law, growers mounted a more subtle challenge by waging a war of attrition designed to wear down the UFW and its supporters. Employer associations published pamphlets and manuals with detailed advice on personnel management and maneuvers that could minimize the law's impact. Attorneys developed expertise in farm labor relations and taught clients how to equivocate and prolong contract negotiations without violating the letter of the law. Growers quickly became adept at stonewalling bargaining sessions, appealing board rulings and decisions, ignoring requests for help during investigations, and otherwise flouting the spirit of the law.

Farm employers also went on the political offensive. The California Farm Bureau Federation launched what became a futile eight-year campaign to have the legislature amend ALRA to conform with the NLRA, the more conservative federal labor statute. Growers rallied behind the 1982 Republican gubernatorial candidate, George Deukmejian, and contributed mightily to his winning campaign. With this one political stroke, growers' anti-ALRA investment finally paid off. Shortly after moving to Sacramento, Deukmejian nearly gutted the act. The new governor installed a pro-grower general counsel who dismissed almost all union complaints and settled make-whole cases involving bad-faith bargaining for lower dollar amounts than had been the rule under the previous regime. Further, Deukmejian slashed the agency's funding, made a string of appointments that reversed the balance of power on the board, and demoted or laid off investigators and administrative law judges.

In the meantime, growers turned to farm labor contractors as another bulwark against the unions. A peculiarity of certain indus-

tries that rely on seasonal and immigrant workers, labor contractors have been a fixture in the agricultural community since Chinese nationals first began hewing the California fields during
the nineteenth century. Contractors serve as middlemen who
match the supply of labor with the demand for labor by recruiting
and managing workers. They organize what is essentially a disor-
ganized market and ensure a modicum of stability and regularity
(Fisher 1953:21), taking a hefty percentage of workers' earnings in
exchange. Although the contractors' numbers and visibility fell
sharply in the 1960s and early 1970s as strong employer associations
and active union hiring halls assumed similar roles, calls for their
services jumped markedly once employers recognized their value
in warding off the union threat.

A quirk in the law enhanced the contractors' appeal. Because
ALRA excludes contractors from the definition of "employer," an
election was required to be held at each work site before union
representation could be established. The act's framers intended
this legal distinction to ensure a degree of accountability and to
deny growers the opportunity to blacklist contractors with pro-
union crews. But instead of protecting workers who wanted to join
a union, this technicality actually undermined union efforts. It
forced the unions into multiple organizing campaigns even though
there might have been significant overlap in the composition of the
work force from farm to farm. It also encouraged growers to dissoci-
ate from all labor relations functions by relegating complete responsibility to contractors who could guarantee nonunion crews.
Over the years, crew leaders have become masterful at screening
out potential union supporters and intimidating workers into anti-
union stances.

The continued influx of immigrants from Mexico, Central America, and Southeast Asia has further stoked the labor contracting
system in California. Contractors are usually of the same ethnicity
as workers and thus have a natural pipeline into the community
here in the United States and back in the sending region or country.
This connection helps contractors locate potential employees and
gives them better control over their crews. New immigrants are
particulary dependent on the contractors, who manage much of
their daily lives and provide some linkage with a remote and alien
outside world. Growers take comfort in the security the contractors
provide, especially when they lack familiarity with the immigrant

workers' language and customs. Unfortunately, the presence of labor contractors is correlated with a high proportion of un-authorized workers and inferior working conditions (Kissam and Griffith 1991:11).

While labor contractors prospered under the tide of immigration, union organizing drives suffered irreversible setbacks. All too often immigrants were used to break strikes by union supporters and to quash burgeoning interest in the union movement. With few alternative resources or skills, immigrants have been willing to cross picket lines and take jobs at low wage rates. Growers' propensity to play off one immigrant group against another dates to the early twentieth century, when growers used recently arrived Hindu workers to undercut the going wage. The situation has barely changed in the intervening years.

As time passed, the unions proved no match for the sophisticated anti-union tactics adopted by some farmers and the virulent hostility expressed by others. The combined effect of growers' antagonism, changes in Sacramento, the reemergence of farm labor contractors, and the continuing oversupply of labor eventually depleted the energies of the farm labor movement. The UFW bore the brunt of these disparate stresses. Since the 1977 jurisdictional agreement with the Teamsters had left field organizing to the UFW, Chavez's union was the only major player in the fields. Thus the UFW became the prime target of the anti-union forces.

The UFW was also undermined from within. Coups, firings, and resignations stripped the union of top-notch legal and organizing talent in the late 1970s. The peace pacts with the Teamsters, which eliminated critical competition, may have engendered complacency and allowed union leaders to focus on legal and political activity at the expense of grass-roots organizing. Moreover, the UFW had trouble adjusting to its role as a labor union. Outsiders and disaffected insiders contend the nitty-gritty of union business did not appeal to Chavez or his colleagues. Victories at the polls were not always converted into signed labor contracts, in part due to employer intransigence and in part to the union's inexperience at the bargaining table. Negotiating sessions often degenerated into bouts of table-pounding and yelling, ideological speeches, and inflexible contract demands. By the early 1980s, the UFW was walking away from some contracts by failing to renegotiate terms when pacts expired.

As of late 1993, the UFW was comparatively quiet and ineffective. Its mission seems to have been redefined and its strategy altered. Leaders of rival unions say the UFW now tends to organize defensively, launching campaigns only after other unions express interest in a site. Its primary activities involve providing services and information, and resuscitating the consumer boycott of table grapes, this time as a protest against the dangers of farmworker exposure to pesticides. Industry spokespeople say the effort has had no impact. The recent death of Chavez has also raised questions about the union's future.

In many respects ALRA has been a disappointment, its intended effect sabotaged by subsequent developments. Despite growers' initial backing of ALRA, they never accommodated to the labor relations system it envisioned and actively fought many of its precepts. The UFW was overwhelmed by exogenous forces and suffered the consequences of its internal problems. Pro-grower bias exhibited by the ALRB during the 1980s no doubt undermined the UFW's confidence and interest in the act. Union leaders claim there was little point in continuing to organize, file election petitions, or initiate unfair labor practice charges once the Deukmejian administration and like-minded Republicans moved in.

Several small unions have continued to organize, however, and occasionally win representation elections. In 1988, for example, the Service Employees' International Union (SEIU) local that represents maintenance and service workers at Stanford University won an election at a fruit and vegetable farm located on university property that employs about fifty-five workers in the peak season. The Creamery Employees and Drivers Local 517 won a number of elections in the early 1990s, as have a few Teamster locals and the Independent Union of Agricultural Workers. On a number of farms where the UFW has been decertified, the surviving workers' committees organized themselves into new independent unions that carry on the collective bargaining relationship. But the tide of union activity has passed and ALRA no longer holds out the promise it once did.

Regional Conditions

Farm unions have failed to make much headway in other states, even though the problems endemic to farmworkers in

California are found throughout the United States. Low wages, erratic employment, inadequate housing, arduous and repetitive physical labor, exposure to chemicals and pesticides, transience, and overbearing bosses are the common facts of life for hundreds of thousands of farmworkers in this country. Whether they work in New York or Arizona, Florida or Michigan, Texas or New Jersey, or any other state with a population of paid seasonal and migrant farm laborers, the stresses and difficulties are ever-present.

Florida. Florida has a substantial population of farmworkers. It is home base for thousands of workers who find agricultural jobs locally during the cooler months but move north in search of additional employment as the temperatures rise. There are approximately two hundred thousand farmworkers in the state. Until 1992, another ten thousand or so Jamaicans came to Florida each year to work the sugarcane harvest under the H-2A program, the federally sanctioned temporary farm labor program. Since 1992, the number of H-2A workers in the state has dropped to about two thousand because many harvest jobs have been mechanized.

Florida's agricultural sector produces a cornucopia of commodities such as citrus fruits, vegetables, livestock and poultry, sugarcane, and nursery ornamentals. Yet farmworkers are in an unenviable situation. The freezes that hit the state during the 1980s destroyed citrus groves and temporarily reduced demand for labor. There are more than two workers for each available farm job and real wages have fallen to levels below those of the late 1960s. Working and living conditions are often deplorable and more than a dozen cases involving alleged peonage have been reported in recent years. Farm labor contractors control about half the supply of farm labor.

A modest show of force in the early 1970s netted the UFW two contracts with citrus operations owned by major corporations. But one company soon extricated itself from the pact by selling off the business. The other, the Minute Maid operations of Coca-Cola, sold some land and whittled its work force to half the number employed when the contract was first signed. Nonetheless, the UFW-Minute Maid relationship has survived and is considered by many farm labor advocates to be an exemplary agreement.

Apart from its involvement at Minute Maid, the UFW has maintained a low profile in Florida, which is a right-to-work state with no strong union tradition. Labor insurgency is rare, and ill-fated efforts to enact a state-level collective bargaining law in 1976 have never been revived.

Some grass-roots organizing is occurring, however. FLOC, the Ohio-based union that represents cucumber and tomato workers in the Midwest, maintains an outpost in the west-central part of Florida where many of its members live in the off-season. FLOC uses the office to cement ties with members by visiting their homes and holding informational meetings about their labor contracts and other union matters. In the long run, FLOC's presence in Florida and its members' familiarity with unions and collective bargaining may inspire other Florida farmworkers to participate in collective action.

The Farmworker Association of Central Florida (FACF) is also organizing farmworkers, but has chosen to focus on a broader agenda that emphasizes group empowerment. The association, led by Tirso Moreno, claims an active membership of more than five thousand Hispanic, Afro-American, and Haitian workers. It enjoys the strong support of Catholic activists and maintains alliances with other farmworker groups, both in Florida and around the country. FACF recently joined a new national coalition called the Farmworkers Network for the Environment and Economic Justice.

The FACF, carefully building its strength and choosing its tactics, is currently expanding into the areas of Immokalee and Homestead, two communities with large populations of settled and migrant farmworkers. FACF is forming leadership groups to involve people in decision making by teaching them to identify issues of concern and then devise action strategies. The association offers a range of social services, including a consumer co-op for food and tools, and the opportunity to bank in a credit union. It has initiated several housing projects, is beginning to lobby for legislative changes that would benefit its members, and is seeking a ban on Benlate, a chemical used in horticulture, until health risks are determined and help is available for workers suffering the ill effects of exposure. Several years ago the association established a workers' co-op that bypasses middlemen by contracting directly with growers to perform harvest and nonharvest jobs. The co-op reaps the profits normally accruing to labor contractors and distributes them among its member-workers.

Ohio. Like many midwestern states, Ohio boasts a large and diverse agricultural sector that encompasses livestock, poultry, and grain. Its farms are moderate in size, averaging slightly less than two hundred acres, and farmers have been quick to mechanize as much of the work as possible. But in the northwestern corner of the state, labor-intensive cash crops such as canning tomatoes and pickle cucumbers predominate. Most of the farms in this area are relatively small, highly profitable family-owned operations that require many seasonal workers.

Each summer some seven thousand migrant workers and their families pour into northwestern Ohio. They come from Florida and Texas to transplant tomatoes, hoe sugar beets, detassle corn, and harvest cucumbers. Many of the migrants, who are primarily Hispanic, return to this region year in and year out and have developed strong ties to individual farms. In an industry sector notorious for its transience, the annual turnover rate in northwestern Ohio is a relatively low thirty percent.

Cucumber pickers are skilled workers. Unlike processing tomatoes, which are harvested mechanically and require minimal labor by anyone who can sort stones and other debris from the gleanings, pickle cucumbers must be harvested manually, with the vines tucked and turned just so to protect the immature fruit from excessive sunlight. Farmworkers and working family members walk up and down the rows every day, picking the fruit precisely when size and degree of ripeness are in harmony. Small, well-shaped cucumbers are highly prized by pickle processors and consumers and generate premium pay for the pickers. Workers earn 50 percent of the gross revenue they generate plus incentive pay based on size and cull rates. Fast, skilled farmworker families often take home $10,000 after a six- or seven-week harvest season.

This unusually cohesive group of migrant farmworkers has also given rise to FLOC, one of the few successful farm labor unions in the country. Under the leadership of Baldemar Velasquez and his father before him, FLOC has chosen to concentrate its efforts on this small and specialized piece of the state's diversified agricultural sector. FLOC has been active in Ohio for almost thirty years and claims a membership of six thousand workers. Since the mid-1980s, FLOC has been party to collectively bargained labor contracts with several dozen cucumber and tomato growers in northwestern Ohio and southeastern Michigan and two national food processors, Campbell Soup Company (which owns the Vlasic pickle brand) and H. J. Heinz Company. More recently, it signed agreements with about eighteen pickle growers and Aunt Jane's and Green Bay, two regional brands owned by Illinois-based processor Dean Foods Company.

FLOC fully exploited the area's industry structure. The financial ties between growers and processors is unusually tight: although growers are free to sell to any buyer, many have supplied the same processor for several generations. FLOC understood this interdependence and realized the only way it would win recognition from growers would be through pressure on the processors. Borrowing a tactic finely honed by his mentor Chavez of the UFW, FLOC president Velasquez launched a consumer boycott against Campbell Soup in 1978.

Although the boycott never threatened Campbell's bottom line, it was sufficiently irritating that seven years later the company convinced many of its allied growers to recognize and bargain with the union. Heinz watched from the sidelines until 1987, when it decided to preempt a product boycott by voluntarily persuading the grower group it bargained with each year over cucumber prices to similarly accept and work with FLOC. The result was a series of multiyear labor contracts involving the union, the growers, and the processors.

The three parties are full participants in an unusual tripartite arrangement that is not founded in federal or state labor statutes. The ad hoc and voluntary understanding depends primarily on the parties' good will and acceptance of the document as a binding contract. Workers have no legal protection when they organize or seek to bargain collectively, nor are there any mechanisms for government protection or enforcement of contract terms except for the possibility of civil litigation for breach of contract. All three parties sign the agreement, although the primary compact exists between the union and the growers. The processors' role is basically to endorse the arrangement by serving as mediators and advocates. They also defray many of the additional costs incurred by growers that arise from the union contract.

The contracts are relatively bare-boned and straightforward. Included are a grievance and arbitration system, clauses pertaining to pesticide control and field sanitation, some recognition of farm seniority in regard to hiring preference, and paid union representatives in the labor camps. Growers are prohibited from making hiring decisions based on workers' union status and FLOC may not require workers to join the union. There is also a rare no-strike/no-lockout provision. (Most union contracts allow for the possibility of a strike or lockout during the life of the agreement under certain narrowly defined circumstances.) The rudiments of a labor relations system are now in place, with strong indications of positive worker-grower interactions. Grievances are typically solved quickly and a few growers appeared as key speakers at the FLOC convention several years ago.

Perhaps the most significant long-term effect of the cucumber contracts is a change in workers' legal status. At the end of the 1993 growing season, cucumber pickers became employees of the growers. The compensation system remains the same but workers are assured of earning the federal minimum wage and receiving benefits from the same social insurance programs available to employees of other types of businesses. This transformation in status is important to cucumber pickers because recent industry protocol has been to treat workers as independent contractors responsible for their own social security contributions and ineligible for unemployment insurance and workers' compensation.

Processors expect that this change in workers' status will add to overall labor costs. Before the 1993 season there were heated discussions about how much more processors would pay for the crop, given growers' new tax liabilities, added paperwork, and increased level of inconvenience. In the end, the parties agreed to a premium of about 10 percent, although this may not be enough to keep the more marginal farms from giving up on pickle cucumbers and opting out of the system.

FLOC, the growers, and the processors nonetheless hope to recoup the added expense through gains in productivity. Heinz, for example, has worked with the union, several of its affiliated growers, and Ohio State University on a multiyear project that focused on productivity-related human resource issues. Researchers tried to discover if productivity rises with experience, if training compensates for lack of experience, and who returns to the same farm each year and why. The answers have provided guidance for worker training and labor-management programs that are geared toward generating productivity improvements. Early results from twenty-five farms where workers received better training netted substantial productivity gains over three years.

New Jersey. Small family farms in New Jersey produce an assortment of labor-intensive crops, including fresh market tomatoes, peppers, cucumbers, asparagus, snap beans, turnips, squash, berries, peaches, and apples. The harvest season runs from late May to November, with the peak occuring during summer. At the height of the season, New Jersey is home to about twenty thousand farmworkers.

New Jersey farmers in need of seasonal labor for years relied on migrant workers, most of whom were single males from Puerto Rico. The Puerto Rican stream dates to the late 1940s when New Jersey growers began recruiting seasonal labor from the island to replace the prisoners of war who had harvested the crops during World War II. About the same time, a contract arrangement involving the U.S. Department of Labor and the Puerto Rican government was established that ostensibly regulated the terms and conditions under which workers could be recruited to work on American farms.

Today the contract system has little sway over the labor market in New Jersey because an informal word-of-mouth network seems to adequately match supply and demand. Growers are also hiring Cambodian and Vietnamese day haulers who come from the Philadelphia/Camden and Trenton areas. A swelling stream of workers from Texas and Mexico is enlarging the state's migrant labor supply and replacing Puerto Rican workers, perceived by many growers as too aggressive in enforcing their rights. Along with the increasing number of Mexican workers has come a steady deterioration in living and working conditions for migrant labor, with numerous reports of minimum wage and other regulatory violations.

Attempts to organize the state's farmworkers have been ongoing since the 1960s. Nonprofit foundations, along with church and social service groups, have tried to organize farm labor both in Puerto Rico and on the mainland. Most of their efforts came to naught. But one indigenous farmworker advocacy group, Comité de Apoyo a los Trabajadores Agrícolas (CATA), emerged in 1979 and successfully advanced the farmworkers' cause on several fronts. CATA lobbied the state legislature for modifications to several laws and challenged farmers' requests for approval to hire temporary foreign workers under the federal H-2A program. As a result of CATA's campaign, farmworkers who log at least 770 hours in a season are now eligible for unemployment insurance. The state minimum wage, which applies to farm employees, is now eighty cents higher than the federal minimum. In addition, petitions for H-2A workers have been rebuffed.

CATA, which claims two thousand members, spun off a sister organization in 1984 named Comité Organizador de Trabajadores Agrícolas (COTA). COTA was intended to function as a labor union, organizing farmworkers and negotiating collective bargaining agreements with growers. But the group has claimed few victories: it has participated in only five representation elections and won a majority of the votes at four sites. So far, COTA has signed just one contract and for several years was mired in litigation on the other three. Wages and working conditions at the one Cumberland County farm under contract are marginally better than at sur-rounding farms. The hourly rate is a few pennies higher than the local average and workers enjoy a number of benefits, including a grievance procedure, paid transportation to and from home if they finish the season, a health and safety committee, and a CATA-sponsored health plan. After a brief hiatus, COTA is once again engaged in quiet, low-key organizing.

Arizona. Arizona is a key producer of several critical crops, such as cotton, winter vegetables, and citrus fruits. Large-scale farming is the norm, with the average farm size about 4,700 acres. There are approximately eighteen thousand paid farmworkers in the state, many of whom are in the United States illegally. Most farmworkers are Mexican nationals, although cohorts from Gua-temala and El Salvador have been growing steadily since the late 1980s.

Like California, Arizona has an agriculture-specific labor rela-tions law that governs union organizing and collective bargaining. But unlike the California law, which provided arguably neutral rules for employer-employee interactions, the Arizona law was an unabashed attempt to throttle union activity just as it started to blossom.

The Arizona Agricultural Employment Relations Act (AAERA) was passed in 1972, at a time when the UFW was aggressively organizing workers and leading strikes in both Arizona and Califor-nia. Although the act permits farm employees to form unions and bargain with employers, it has an overt pro-grower bias. For exam-ple, workers are eligible to vote in a representation election only if they worked for the same employer in the preceding calendar year. Given the high turnover in agricultural jobs, this provision severely restricts workers' right to accept or reject union representation. AAERA also limits workers' right to strike, a constraint the act justifies by noting the seasonal and perishable nature of agricultural produce. Strikes can be called only following a secret ballot vote and growers may obtain a temporary injunction against the strike if they agree to submit the dispute to binding arbitration. Growers may also secure restraining orders against union pickets during organizing drives and they have no obligation to provide access to workers lodged on their property.

Union organizing in Arizona has fallen off sharply in the last two decades. UFW activity flared but then died out during the early 1970s. In 1974–75 a disastrous citrus strike in Yuma drove a sharp wedge between local Mexican-American farmworkers, Mexican workers who legally commuted over the border from Sonora to their jobs, and illegal immigrants from Mexico, all of whom viewed the strike from wildly different perspectives and experienced its consequences differently (Sanchez and Romo 1981:1). Union organizers regrouped in 1977 and founded the Maricopa County Organizing Project (MCOP), whose strategy called for ignoring the legal distinctions among farmworkers and organizing around the issues of human and civil rights. In 1979, after two years of building a movement and an infrastructure of worker committees, the organization ceded its identity to the newly formed Arizona Farm Workers Union (AFWU). The union focused its energies primarily on undocumented workers and even tried organizing in the Mexican communities that were sending workers to the state. In time, the union secured three contracts.

Today, several small unions represent a few hundred workers at a handful of sites. But organizing activity is at a standstill. The discouraging impact of the AAERA and the absence of strong, committed leaders among the farmworkers has taken its toll. Moreover, the UFW is effectively barred from operating within the state by a multimillion dollar judgment imposed a few years ago following an illegal secondary boycott against one employer; any dues the union collects could be garnisheed by the wronged grower. A more serious problem for the union, however, is potential bankruptcy if the award is upheld on appeal.

New York. Absent official surveys that accurately quantify the number of hired farmworkers in New York, most estimates peg the population at about forty thousand. Migrant and seasonal workers handle the bulk of the harvest chores on the state's fruit and vegetable farms and probably account for two-thirds of the total

number of farm laborers; full-time farm and dairy workers constitute the remainder. Although New York's agricultural sector ranks
well behind such powerhouses as California, Florida, and Texas,
farming is critical to the state's economy. The cash value of farm
produce reached almost $3 billion in 1989 and agriculture sustains
thousands of jobs throughout the state. New York is also among the
leading U.S. producers of apples, milk, cauliflower, lettuce, and
sweet corn.

Migrant workers are invaluable to local fruit and vegetable farmers. Most workers enter the state for the summer and fall harvest,
with a few arriving early for spring cleanup and planting and others
extending their stay into late fall to finish out the cabbage and
squash harvest or to earn extra cash in the flourishing nursery
sector. Seasonal employment peaks in early to mid-September
when the apple crop is ready to come in. Most of the state's migrant
workers make their homes in Florida or Texas, with a not insignificant few coming north from Mexico, Central America, and Puerto
Rico. For the first forty years after World War II, Afro-Americans
made up the majority of migrants. But since the early 1980s, Haitians who settled in Florida have made their way north and the
proportion of Hispanic farmworkers has increased dramatically.

During the late summer and fall, New York is also temporary
home to almost three thousand workers from Jamaica. These men
enter the state each year under the federal H-2A program to help
harvest apples, mostly in the Hudson and Champlain valleys and
throughout the Lake Ontario corridor of the state. For years New
York was the second largest user of H-2A workers in the country,
ranking well behind Florida. Given the sharp dropoff in H-2A
workers in that state, New York has now claimed the number one
slot.

Living and working conditions for the state's farm labor force
have improved slightly over the years. New York is one of nineteen
states that include farmworkers under state minimum wage laws,
and its statute nominally insures that workers' pay keeps pace with
the federal minimum wage. The state has promulgated standards
for labor camps that house five or more persons, including at least
one farmworker. New York requires employers to provide fresh
drinking water where at least four workers are employed. A migrant
labor contractor registration act stipulates that crew leaders must
register with the state and supply information on wages, housing,

and working conditions, and that workers must receive a written wage agreement from the farmer/employer. Farmers in some parts of the state are voluntarily upgrading the housing stock and generally taking more care about managing the work force, at least in part because they are experiencing difficulty in attracting and retaining productive workers. This tendency is most noticeable among dairy farmers, who bemoan the lack of skilled workers and occasionally try to compensate with wages and benefits that almost match those offered by nonfarm employers.

But most farmworkers in New York experience lives fraught with stress and uncertainty. Medical and dental care is woefully inadequate, all too many workers live in rundown housing, and host communities are rife with racism. State laws reflect a false dichotomy between the farm and nonfarm sectors and thus do not go far enough in protecting farmworkers. Like their peers elsewhere, New York farmworkers are excluded from most protective labor legislation, such as mandatory day-of-rest and overtime-pay requirements, and they generally do not qualify for programs such as disability and unemployment insurance because strict eligibility standards tend to preclude agricultural workers. Even where statutes do apply, some deceitful farm employers take full advantage of the loopholes or simply evade the laws entirely, knowing full well that enforcement measures are weak and ineffective.

Perhaps the most significant problems confronting the state's migrant farmworkers are due to the impermanence of their jobs. Although hourly and piece-rate wages are relatively low, efficient workers on productive farms can earn upward of $400 a week. This would be an acceptable level of income but for the fact that farmwork is notoriously unsteady. Given the variability of the weather, uneven crop maturation, the chances of becoming sick, and miscellaneous failures to report for work, few employees actually clock enough time or pick enough crops to earn that much money consistently. The income problem is compounded when workers return to their home bases during the cooler months of the year and cannot find steady employment there either.

Vibrant and sustained farm union activity in New York is almost nonexistent. The work force is racially and ethnically diverse, geographically scattered, relatively docile, and short on charismatic leaders. A few organizers, with the support of the church-affiliated Migrant Ministry, are laying the groundwork in the Hudson Valley for what could ultimately become a labor union by sponsoring soccer leagues and setting up consumer co-ops. In other parts of the state, small groups of migrant workers periodically stage sponta- neous work actions over such issues as unfair firings, minimum wage violations, unpaid wages, evictions, and erratic scheduling. One group of duck workers, mostly undocumented immigrants from Central America, recently secured $20,000 in back wages just as the employer was preparing to sell the operation and leave the country. But by and large, such incidents have been isolated and relatively ineffectual.

And Elsewhere . . . The situation in New York is not unlike that experienced by farmworkers in other parts of the country. Mush- room pickers, laboring under dank, dark, and high-pressure condi- tions in large warehouses in a corner of southeastern Pennsylvania, recently went on the offensive. Workers at one of the larger farms staged a wildcat strike in April 1993, in protest over a new and ostensibly reduced wage scale (*New York Times* May 23, 1993). The walkout by 140 Mexican workers, slightly more than one-quarter of the company's labor force, lasted three weeks. It generated substan- tial publicity, attracted a fair amount of community support, and led to the group's affiliation with Local 1034 of the Retail, Whole- sale and Department Store Union (RWDSU), which represents about one hundred workers in two nearby mushroom canneries.

Although the wage issue remained unresolved, the union called off the strike so workers who had not been dismissed for trespassing or who had not found other jobs could return to the mushrooms. Meanwhile, the RWDSU took advantage of a series of state court rulings which have held that mushroom workers are engaged in horticulture, not agriculture, and so are protected by the Pennsylva- nia Labor Relations Act. The local filed a petition for a representa- tion election, which was held in late May 1993. Assuming the union won majority support, survives any legal challenges surrounding the election, and successfully negotiates a labor contract, it will have gained a foothold in a small but important sector of the industry.

What makes this situation especially intriguing is the interest it has aroused in the RWDSU to pursue an organizing campaign among the local mushroom workers, who number about twenty-five hundred. Moreover, the incident prompted a state legislator to introduce a bill that would allow farmworkers throughout the state to petition for representation elections and bargain collectively under the aegis of the state's labor relations act. The bill's supporters are hopeful it will eventually pass both houses and be signed into law.

In other regions of the United States, small independent unions occasionally rise up and win a victory here and there. The Border Agricultural Workers Union, based in El Paso, Texas, won a contract with a New Mexico chili grower in 1991 after twenty-two work stoppages that involved hundreds of workers and daily protests (Commission on Security and Cooperation in Europe 1993:28). And an independent organizer who travels the country in an effort to build a vibrant labor movement among farmworkers is planning an organizing campaign among fruit pickers and packers in Arizona.

Apart from these few examples, most farmworkers remain isolated and divided, without leaders or legal protections. Farmworkers have little reason to expect that conditions will change and improve in their lifetimes.

4. Constraints and Opportunities

The fight seems to have been knocked out of many American workers. Factories are closing, foreign imports are rising, wages are barely keeping pace with the cost of living, benefits are dwindling. Worry, anxiety, and concern about jobs and the future are ever-present in Americans' minds. Surprisingly, few workers are finding succor in the union movement. Perhaps the mistrust of unions that so pervades our political-economic discourse deters them. Perhaps the deterministic belief that only a miracle can revive the type of economic growth that once sustained millions of well-paying industrial jobs now saps their interest in unions. Perhaps the sophisticated union-busting strategies adopted by employers depletes their energies. Whatever the reason, the level and intensity of union organizing drives has diminished markedly over the last ten years.

The farm sector is no different. With but a few exceptions, farm labor insurgency is rare these days. The UFW, a few Teamsters locals, and several independent farmworker unions have occasionally won representation elections in California. Since the 1988–89 fiscal year, the ALRB has held fewer than twenty-five elections a year, including many decertification elections. In the Ohio area, FLOC recently negotiated an agreement with the growers and two brands associated with Dean Foods Company and continues organizing the region's farmworkers.

Although farmworkers occasionally join unions, stage work stoppages, and try to negotiate labor contracts with employers, the farm labor movement is in stasis. The UFW has turned its attention from

68

grass-roots organizing to providing services and reviving the once-potent consumer boycott. With the death of Chavez, the union's founding president and powerful symbol, its future as a labor organization is far from certain. COTA, the union that organized Puerto Rican farmworkers in New Jersey, briefly declared a moratorium out of frustration with a cloudy legal environment. In other locales, farmworker activism is stymied by a host of inhibiting factors, including the indifference of the larger community, the absence of indigenous leadership, geographic dispersion, lack of financial resources, an excess supply of labor, unsupportive labor laws, and employer resistance.

Such obstacles have been ubiquitous for years and have certainly made union organizing among farmworkers more challenging and less fruitful than among nonfarm workers in this country. Organizing unions and winning labor contracts has always been difficult in the United States. But ever since the passage of the NLRA in 1935, workers' ongoing and strategically focused actions have netted recognition and signed agreements with thousands of employers. Farmworkers' efforts, by contrast, have been far more sporadic and largely unsuccessful.

Farmworkers are hard to organize. They are stratified socially and economically, thereby constituting an almost random assemblage of labor force attachment, skill levels, race, and ethnicity. Unpaid family members, full-time and skilled workers, and casual and seasonal "unskilled" workers are all part of the farmworker population. There are Caucasians and Afro–Americans, immigrants from Latin America, the Caribbean, the Middle East, and Southeast Asia, and temporary contract workers from abroad. Some farmworkers belong to relatively stable communities and others are migrants who come and go with the harvest. Many are illegal immigrants desperate for anonymity and work, and many possess little knowledge of the English language or American laws and culture. Some work and live among dozens or even hundreds of companions while others labor in small isolated groups spread over a vast rural landscape.

Most of the preconditions that have proven necessary for sustained union activity in this country are absent in the agricultural sector. Models of organizing and collective bargaining have evolved to reflect the realities of industry, commerce, service, and government, where the workforce is relatively fixed, homogeneous, permanent, and easily accessible.

Where the labor force, labor market, industry structure, and terms of employment deviate from the paradigm, however, organized labor's interest typically flags and many of its efforts break down. Low-wage immigrant workers who increasingly fill such diverse jobs as janitor, seamstress, garment cutter, hospital orderly, shellfish shucker, and chicken cleaner are almost as difficult to organize as migrant and seasonal farmworkers. They experience many of the same indignities and much of the same exploitation as their agricultural counterparts. They, too, work in industries whose labor markets are characterized by high turnover and a surplus of labor. Like farmworkers, many of these nonfarm workers are undocumented and their kinship networks control recruitment for many jobs, with certain ethnic groups often associated with particular tasks. As in agriculture, where labor intermediaries and packinghouse/marketing associations and food processors obscure issues of ownership and control, workers in many low-wage sectors may never know who their employer really is: the contractor, the jobber, the brand name manufacturer, or the final consumer of the service.

Unions have not yet learned how to organize under these conditions. They are stymied by logistical constraints and legal complications. Their activists and staff members are often unfamiliar with the immigrants' language and customs. Rarely do they encounter employers who welcome the union. And vestiges of racism may dull the unions' interest and concern. Organizing conditions in the farm sector are arguably more discouraging than in the service or manufacturing sectors, and workers are not even protected by the NLRA. Where, then, do farmworkers find the incentive to fight?

Fierce employer opposition to unions is endemic to American labor history. This attitude has taken on a particularly virulent and repressive cast among farmers. The farm lobby succeeded in exempting agriculture from the NLRA and has scuttled efforts to secure organizing and collective bargaining rights for farmworkers in several states. Indeed, the unique status claimed by farmers and conferred on them by statute and regulation has made their enmity toward unions extraordinarily difficult to circumvent.

Traditionally, farmers have regarded themselves—and have been perceived by many Americans—as the embodiment of the virtues on which this country was founded. They stand before us as proud tillers of the soil whose small family farms anchor society. They symbolize democracy and self-reliance, and just so happen to help satisfy the nation's appetite. Although this romantic myth does not bear up under scrutiny, given the growing prominence of powerful marketing cooperatives and impersonal corporate farms, it nonetheless buoys farmers' union animus.

But underneath the farm community's seeming self-righteousness lies a more genuine rationale for its anti-union sentiments: money and control. Because the harvest is a make-or-break proposition for most farmers, many fear that a strike at the height of the season would cause irreversible financial ruin. Farmers generally seethe at the thought that union leaders with no commitment to any particular farm, and workers who come and go through the years, should have any influence over their profits, let alone any input into wages and working conditions. They also insist that intense foreign and domestic competition prevent them from paying the higher wages and providing the fringe benefits that unions invariably demand.

There may be some logic and reason behind the farmers' stance. Yet the claims of farmworkers carry equal force and validity. Migrant and seasonal farmworkers in particular are among the most vulnerable groups in American society. They work long, hard hours, earn low annual incomes, live in shabby and sometimes unsafe surroundings, and have little voice or presence in the social and political arena. Attempts by federal, state, and local governments to regulate, and thereby improve, farmworkers' living and working conditions are often inadequate, indifferent, and minimally enforced. Workers' complaints about and legal proceedings against recalcitrant employers frequently result in firings, harassment, and years of delay and uncertainty before matters are resolved. In short, farmworkers who want to do something about their lives have few viable options.

A long-standing tenet of labor relations theory (and one proven by practice in the nonfarm sectors of the economy) holds that workers benefit by forming unions and bargaining with employers over wages and terms of employment. Farmworker unions, however, serve as an unfortunate counterexample. For the most part, they have yet to achieve durable gains for their members. Nor have they sustained themselves over time as effective and functioning institutions. Unfortunately, the short-term prospects for farm labor unions, and farmworkers themselves, are not promising.

There are still fundamental obstacles to successful farm labor organizing and the evolution of enduring and vibrant farm labor unions. Consider, for example, the impact of thousands of illegal immigrants who pour over the southern United States border each year or the effect of linguistic, cultural, and racial diversity within the farmworker population. Farm labor contractors, migrancy, demoralization, and inadequate legal protections also inhibit and depress the farm labor movement.

Labor Market Issues

Supply. Plentiful, cheap labor has been a staple of American agriculture for most of the last century. Waves of immigrants from Asia and Latin America, white Americans displaced by drought and economic depressions, Afro–Americans from the South forced to migrate to find work, and thousands of temporary foreign workers have sustained an enormously productive agricultural sector. The situation is similar today, as eager farm employers welcome the thousands of legal and illegal immigrants, and the domestic workers and temporary foreign workers who continuously replenish the pool of farm labor.

The supply of workers exceeds the demand, despite occasional gaps in the labor supply, such as occur among dairy farmers in New York, who contend there is a shortage of skilled and experienced full-time workers. In the states with the largest farm sectors and the greatest need for farmworkers, people outnumber jobs by at least two to one. Labor economists estimate that there are two to three farmworkers for each farm job in Florida while only half of California's more than 750,000 farmworkers are employed at any given time.

During the 1980s, when Congress was debating what ultimately became IRCA, farm lobbyists fought hard to avoid losing their low-cost work force to tighter immigration controls. In time, all parties agreed to a compromise farm-specific piece of the legislation known as the Special Agricultural Workers (SAW) program. Under SAW, the federal government offered amnesty to illegal immigrants who could prove they had worked in seasonal agricultural jobs in the United States during the twelve months that ended on May 1, 1986. The statute also contained a provision—the Replenishment Agricultural Workers (RAW) program—that guaranteed farm employers would not lose short-term access to a sufficient supply of labor. RAW obligated the federal government to allow additional farm workers into the country during fiscal 1990–93 if the secretaries of labor and agriculture determined a labor shortage existed. The RAW program lapsed in September 1993 without having been activated.

The motivation behind IRCA was to curtail illegal immigration by imposing sanctions on employers who hired unauthorized aliens. Congressional intent notwithstanding, IRCA *enlarged* the supply of farm labor and did little to check the flow of immigration. The Immigration and Naturalization Service (INS) originally predicted that anywhere from 400,000 to 800,000 undocumented farmworkers would file for legal status under the SAW program. In fact, about 1.3 million people applied and INS approved almost all the requests. Although growers initially feared that SAW workers would exit the industry and precipitate a labor shortage, the opposite has occurred. Most SAW beneficiaries continue to work the fields and reap the harvest. Language barriers, family ties, and lack of transferable skills bind many SAW beneficiaries to agriculture.

Predictions that tighter controls on immigration and employer sanctions would constrict the farm labor supply have not been borne out. America's borders are as porous as ever, and the persistent influx of immigrants, legal and otherwise, provides a constant source of labor. Dire economic and political conditions in Mexico, Central America, and Southeast Asia still propel distraught and hungry people to seek haven in this country. IRCA has not made this quest any more elusive. Obtaining the relevant documents to support a work application is also a simple procedure. According to farm labor experts, illegal immigrants can buy fraudulent documents openly on the streets for as little as thirty or thirty-five dollars.

Many of these newcomers turn to agriculture as a source of income. Entry into the farm labor market is comparatively easy for people with few skills and little experience in American society. Highly articulated networks of family and friends continuously recruit new workers for jobs in the direct employ of farmers or in a contractor's crew. For people whose false documents require them to seek shelter in a milieu where they blend in, farm work in a locale with high concentrations of immigrants is a necessity. Clearly, the pressures of excess supply are most keenly felt in the border states, where wages and working conditions are especially grim. Real wages in California dropped precipitously during the 1980s; one study reports they fell 13 percent during the first five post-IRCA years compared to a 2 percent decline nationally (Commission on Agricultural Workers 1992:93–94).

The chronic oversupply of labor has been, and continues to be, a key impediment to farm labor organizing. Attempts to organize unions in an environment where workers are cheap and abundant is often futile. Agricultural workers are close substitutes for each other; although many specialize by crop, the labor they perform is relatively unskilled and quickly mastered. Employers thus have their pick of job seekers, a situation that limits their patience for naysayers and dissidents. Workers invariably understand the unspoken rules and become wary of doing anything that might arouse the employer's ire and lead to dismissal. There is always a line of unemployed workers willing and eager to take a vacated job.

Organizing tactics such as strikes, picketing, leafletting, and even relatively innocuous house meetings, can be easily subverted by a supply-heavy labor market. Growers throughout California have defeated numerous union organizing drives over the years by trucking in strikebreakers, firing union sympathizers, and otherwise ignoring or repressing union activities without having to sacrifice the harvest or their farms.

In recent years, certain provisions in IRCA have only reinforced farmworkers' seeming acceptance of working conditions and indifference to union overtures. Despite monetary sanctions for hiring illegal immigrants, employers/farmers are under no obligation to authenticate workers' immigration or amnesty papers. Some farmers, whether knowingly or not, hire illegal immigrants. These workers are especially reluctant to complain, express their opinions, or join a union for fear their words and actions will attract the attention of the farmer and ultimately the immigration service. Unwilling to risk deportation, workers tend to accept the status quo.

Union organizing can make little headway when people are scared, passive, and desperate for work. Worker solidarity, a vital component in building a labor union, is difficult to achieve if workers worry about their livelihood and resent peers who unwittingly depress already low wage rates. Unions have no leverage over employers in such circumstances because they cannot depend on workers to take direction from or maintain their commitment to a union.

Worker Heterogeneity. The farmworker population has always comprised a vast assortment of ethnic and racial groups, including but not limited to Chinese, Japanese, Pakistanis, Filipinos, Mexicans, Native Americans, Afro–Americans, Haitians, Portuguese, Jamaicans, Puerto Ricans, and Yemenis. Lately, Guatemalan Indians and Mexicans from the cities and several remote states are entering this country and adding still more variety to the polyglot pool of farm labor.

Labor force heterogeneity remains an obstacle to farmworker unions. Shrewd farmers often played off one group of workers against another. During the 1930s, for example, the California State Relief Administration reported that farmers preferred a mixed-nationality work force " 'to prevent mutual understanding among the workers which would lead to labor solidarity, to collective action' " (Fisher 1953:32). Today, Afro–American farmworkers in New York speak disparagingly about their Hispanic peers, whom they perceive to be monopolizing jobs by selling their labor cheap.

By contrast, the relative homogeneity of the California farm labor force during the 1960s and 1970s facilitated union organizing. The UFW succeeded in rallying thousands of farmworkers behind its banner in part by building on the dominant Hispanic culture and Catholic religion. Although Chavez ultimately lost the support of the Filipino cohort, which felt excluded from the fabric of the UFW's life, he helped a community coalesce among the region's Mexican and Mexican-American farmworkers. Once that occurred, Chavez masterfully forged links between the group's particular concerns about tangible matters such as wages, health care, and job safety and more abstract issues such as social and economic justice.

Replicating Chavez's feat in the current environment is difficult, even in California. Would-be organizers are daunted by the number of unknown languages and cultural mores among the most recent immigrants: the growing numbers of Mexican Indians who do not speak Spanish, the refugees from various Asian countries, the workers from the Middle East and the Caribbean. Such diversity inhibits the evolution of cohesive groups with shared values and goals. Indeed, ethnic and racial distinctions are often cited as a critical explanation for the dearth of union organizing among farmworkers in New York, where the migrant population consists of Afro–Americans, Haitians, Mexican-Americans, Central Americans, Puerto Ricans, and Filipinos. Although relations among the assorted groups seem peaceful on the surface, cultural biases and long-range interests differ markedly.

Farm Labor Contractors. Labor contractors are a peculiarity of certain industries that rely on seasonal and immigrant workers. They have been vital to the agricultural community since Chinese nationals first began working the California fields in the 1860s. Contractors are the middlemen who recruit and manage labor, and who match the supply of farmworkers with the demand for farmworkers. Federal and state governments also maintain employment services that try to match workers and jobs within or across state lines, but these facilities are often bypassed by workers and employers who dislike the accompanying scrutiny and paperwork. In the absence of alternative private or public institutions that could efficiently allocate farm labor, contractors perform a key function.

Unfortunately, labor contractors have frequently proved to be unsavory characters who take advantage of workers' vulnerability. The Japanese farm labor contractors based in California in the early 1900s were one notable exception. These men served as both labor union and employer association by fostering a social infrastructure that quickly led to the economic and entrepreneurial prosperity of their ethnic brothers. In general, though, contractors have a reputation for exploiting and abusing farmworkers, and for paying lower wages and providing worse living conditions than farmers who hire workers directly. Federal laws such as the Farm Labor Contractor Registration Act of 1964 (FLCRA) and the Migrant and Seasonal Agricultural Worker Protection Act of 1983 (MSAWPA) were enacted specifically to curb the mistreatment of farmworkers and to thwart the spread of the contracting system.

In California, farm labor contractors' visibility and activity did indeed decline during the 1960s and 1970s. But this condition prevailed only so long as the UFW and strong employer associations assumed the contractors' role as recruiters and managers of labor. Once the UFW's influence began to wane and employer associations cast off their labor-related functions, contractors reemerged as key players in the market. Their number has grown exponentially since IRCA was passed, resulting in fierce competition for grower contracts and slim profit margins for the contractors.

The situation is similar in other major agricultural states. Labor contractors reportedly control access to about half the farm jobs in Florida. In Texas, workers apparently find jobs in winter vegetable harvesting only after joining a contractor's crew. In a prime fruit-growing region in upstate New York, one innovative labor contractor finds jobs for approximately 850 workers and provides much-needed harvest labor for scores of farmers. By recruiting mostly Hispanic workers for his crews, this particular contractor has further shifted the ethnic balance of the migrant and seasonal labor force, once the exclusive preserve of Haitians and Afro–Americans.

Indeed, as immigration continues to surge, the market's need for labor contractors intensifies. Contractors typically arise from among the various ethnic, linguistic, and cultural groups and are thus well positioned to manage their crews and recruit additional workers. Short on cash, miles from home, and marooned in inhospitable surroundings, new immigrants in particular are dependent on the contractors and are exceedingly malleable. Not surprisingly, the ubiquity of labor contractors seems to spread and working conditions tend to deteriorate as the number of illegal immigrants in an area rises.

Union organizing in an environment dominated by labor contractors is well-nigh impossible. Fully aware of farmers' aversion to unions, contractors secure their ties with growers by ensuring their crews remain union-free.

Ironically, certain provisions in state and federal statutes foster demand for the contractors' services. ALRA, the California farm labor law, provided farmers with a loophole that could guarantee nonunion crews. The 1986 immigration act further reinforced the tilt toward labor contractors. Although IRCA takes the opposite approach from ALRA and considers contractors to be employers, the net effect has been the same. Farmers are eager to hand off IRCA's paperwork requirements to contractors as well as the legal responsibility for abiding by (or violating) its provisions. The result: labor contractors are proliferating, especially in California and Florida. In the citrus groves of Ventura County, California, for example, there are dozens of contractors where twenty years ago there were but one or two.

Industry Characteristics

Physical Realities. Farming in America is, by and large, a solitary affair. Farmers and their families till, sow, and reap the fields in relative isolation from their neighbors. Farmsteads are scattered about the countryside, sometimes separated by a road, oftentimes by acres of private property. Even in primary agricultural states such as California and Florida, where large corporate farms dominate certain regions, sites are typically remote.

For migrant and seasonal farmworkers, the physical setting defines the parameters of their social lives. In many locales where farmers provide housing or some form of rudimentary shelter for short-term employees, workers are usually placed in secluded camps on growers' property. Most workers lack private transportation and on-site telephone service is rare. Workers occasionally go into town but then have no place to congregate. This situation makes it hard for people to communicate and share concerns about work and ideas about unions.

Successful union organizing depends heavily on peer interaction, and on the ability of one or several committed and articulate people to rouse the interest and desire of their colleagues for a union. Momentum generally builds like an inverted pyramid and ultimately requires a critical mass for a movement to really take hold. When workers live in scattered camps of five or even twenty-five people, and are basically incommunicado save for an occasional trip to the nearby market or tavern, union organizing is painstaking. Union campaigns have shown promise in parts of California where workers enjoy social interaction in open, settled communities. But such conditions do not ensure success. Organizing drives have foundered in Florida despite living arrangements similar to those in California.

A related problem is the difficulty professional union organizers have in reaching migrant and seasonal workers who are sequestered on growers' property. Employers are notoriously protective of their property rights and frequently refuse passage to outsiders. On numerous occasions, farmers have harassed and sometimes assaulted labor advocates who attempted to visit employees, even during nonwork hours. In 1971, the New Jersey Supreme Court took the unusual step of modifying the state's common law on property rights to allow lawyers, social workers, and union organizers access to farmworkers in farm labor camps. Such access is indispensable to union efforts in an environment where workers have limited contact with the outside world.

The open fields characteristic of most farming regions in the United States also inhibit traditional organizing tactics. Passing out union leaflets, newsletters, or other printed materials is difficult when workers do not enter or leave the worksite through a few doors or gates on a fixed schedule as they do in factories. Likewise, locating workers to notify them of union meetings or a work action is problematic when employers move workers from field to field without notice. Mounting picket lines and sustaining strikes is futile when strikebreakers can cross the line simply by entering the field from any number of places.

Seasonality. About 65 percent of the farmwork in this country is performed by farmer/owners and unpaid family members. The rest of the work is done by hired employees, including full-time and part-time, and seasonal and migrant labor. The seasonal and migrant workers, however, constitute the bulk of the hired labor force. These workers are in great demand during the harvest and sometimes for a short period before and after, but are summarily laid off when the season is over. Although some farm labor economists contend that migrancy was diminishing, the passage of IRCA seems to have reversed that trend (Commission on Security and Cooperation in Europe 1993:13).

Given the short duration of many farms jobs, few workers remain in one spot long enough to develop the attachments and connections needed to sustain union activity. Intra-season turnover on farms is high and workers often do not return to the same employer from one year to the next. Just as geographic dispersion tends to undermine union organizing, so too does seasonal employment and transience. Committed and veteran workers who can carry the organizing burden are hard to find when the work force is in constant flux.

Sociopolitical Realities. Farm labor advocates say that years of economic and political powerlessness, and the scarcity of viable employment alternatives have taken their toll on farm laborers. They work erratically, earn low annual incomes, perform jobs shunned by the rest of the population, and lack a forceful lobby in Washington and state capitals. Many migrant and seasonal workers seem to accept the status quo and see no hope for change or improvement. Service providers who work with Hispanic migrants in New York, for example, say this population is relatively docile and prefers to fit in rather than try to change what the workers regard as given.

With a few notable exceptions, farmworkers have yet to form cohesive, well-identified, enduring groups. One reason is surely their ethnic and racial diversity. Another is their near-invisible status in American society. Analogously, only a few grass-roots leaders have emerged who could appeal to their colleagues' pride, give voice to their concerns, and motivate their energy. Although some labor advocates argue that professional organizers are necessary to guide the early stages of a union campaign, they hasten to add that groups must eventually produce their own leaders and coalesce into cohesive units before labor solidarity can be achieved and sustained.

In recent years, farmworkers have received little encouragement or support from American society. The fertile social and political conditions that nourished Chavez and the UFW during the 1960s and 1970s are noticeably absent. The clamor for social justice and the desire to throw off old strictures and adopt norms of empowerment have been eclipsed by more individualized concerns. The issues that fired the collective imagination of our society twenty-five years ago have receded. And farmworkers, along with other vulnerable and unprotected groups, no longer claim society's sympathy. There are no students queuing up to work for the unions, few church or social advocacy groups pleading the farmworkers' cause. Even the UFW's revived consumer boycott against table grapes has failed to attract much of a following.

Mainstream labor organizations continue to exhibit the same ambivalence that has always characterized their attitude toward farmworker unions. A series of farm unions chartered by the AFL and CIO in the post–World War II years came and went, but accomplished little. Organizing tactics drawn from industry, such as calling strikes and narrowly focusing on wages while ignoring the absence of group solidarity, undermined union efforts. The enmity of employers and surrounding communities toward unionization and repression by local authorities also hindered the union movement. Red-baiting, injunctions, jailings, and violence marked many union campaigns well into the 1970s.

Organized labor's commitment to farmworkers today is unclear. The logistical difficulties of organizing a dispersed, migrant population, the lack of familiarity with the industry and with the workers' languages and customs, and the workers' seeming indifference toward unions discourage outreach attempts. Although labor leaders express concern that farmworkers are excluded from federal and most state statutes that grant nonfarm employees the right to form unions and bargain collectively, they are not rushing to commit the financial and staff resources needed to foster the spread of union activity.

Legal Matters

Right to Organize. Farmworkers are one of the few occupational groups in the United States without the protected right to form unions and bargain collectively over wages and terms of employment. They are excluded from the NLRA, which guarantees most other private-sector employees the protected right to organize and negotiate with management. Only a handful of states—including Arizona, California, Hawaii, Idaho, Kansas, and Wisconsin—have extended these protections to farmworkers, either through generic labor relations laws or agriculture-specific statutes.

Farmworkers are not prohibited from organizing themselves into unions and bargaining through self-chosen representatives. But in most states they have no legal forum for pressing their case or challenging unilateral employer actions. Some union leaders contend the absence of legal structures that protect and regulate farm labor organizing seriously impedes union activity.

Union activists are free to pursue their cause even without a legal framework, as organizers did in some industries in the years before the NLRA was enacted. But labor advocates suggest that farmworkers would be more likely to support a union crusade if they had legal protection against employers' wrath. Workers today seem to want the security of knowing there are laws (even if perfunctorily enforced) against summary firings of employees who engage in concerted activity or express pro-union sympathies. They may also want some assurance that their efforts will be rewarded, that farmers will be obliged to recognize a union election victory and at least sit down at the bargaining table.

The absence of legal structures has not entirely impeded the farm union movement, however. Farm labor activism has rallied some workers intermittently since the late nineteenth century. Small crop- and region-specific unions appeared in states as diverse as California, Illinois, Colorado, Montana, and New Jersey. Some units grew out of spontaneous strikes and others reflected determined organizing by grass-roots leaders or professional organizers. In 1933, for example, almost fifty-seven thousand field workers participated in sixty-one strikes in seventeen states (Jamieson[1945] 1976:16).

Agricultural Labor Relations Act. Despite the excitement and optimism that attended the enactment of ALRA in 1975, the act has not spawned a vibrant or durable farm labor movement either in California or elsewhere in the United States. ALRA has been a mixed blessing for farm union organizing. Aside from recognizing workers' unambiguous right to form unions and bargain collectively and obliging the ALRB to follow precedent set by the federal NLRA wherever appropriate, ALRA embodies provisions that reflect the distinctive characteristics of agriculture. Nonetheless, the law contains several conceptual flaws that blunt its impact. Even the UFW, which was a critical player in the act's creation, no longer espouses collective bargaining legislation as a primary goal for the farm labor movement.

In spite of its deficiencies, several provisions in the act have been lauded by labor advocates as advancing and safeguarding the interests of workers.

- The law's preamble is worded such that labor experts say it commits the state to actively encourage collective bargaining between farm labor and management. (In the early days of ALRA, for example, ALRB staff members held sessions to educate farmworkers about their rights under the law.)
- ALRA adopts a relatively tolerant view of secondary boycotts against a neutral employer. It prohibits them as a tool to force employer recognition of a union, but allows them as a way to inform the public about labor disputes with an employer and to ask consumers to cease patronizing businesses that distribute the employer's product so long as the information conveyed is truthful and the union is a certified representative of the employer's workers. Under the NLRA, by contrast, courts have held that unions may not request consumers to withdraw their patronage from a neutral, or secondary, employer.
- There is no voluntary union recognition by employers under ALRA, a provision that eliminates the potential for sweetheart deals between employers and unions, and minimizes the value of the boycott as a pressure tactic.
- The act pays attention to timeliness by requiring elections within seven days after a petition is filed or within forty-eight hours if a strike is in progress. Similarly, employer objections to an election are reserved for post-election hearings in order to prevent the delays that arise when employers can object and force hearings before an election is held.

- Under ALRA, farmers are obliged to make whole for wages and benefits employees lose due to bad-faith bargaining. This provision stands in sharp contrast to the NLRA, which merely allows the NLRB to issue an order requiring the employer to bargain in good faith but stipulates no penalty for failure to comply.

Despite the careful attention that went into crafting what many proponents hoped would be the perfect labor law, ALRA contains several flaws.

- The absence of deadlines or time limits means administrative and procedural delays often result in cases that drag on for years.
- Separating the liability and remedy phases of an unfair labor practice case prolongs its resolution, adds to the expense of prosecuting and defending, and minimizes the chances that justice will be done.
- Power is concentrated in the ALRB's general counsel, who has the authority to dismiss or accept complaints, settle or sue, stonewall the act or vigorously implement it.
- Because union certification is retained until employees actively initiate decertification proceedings, control of a bargaining unit's destiny rests entirely with workers who may not understand the intricacies of decertification or who may fear union retaliation if they seek decertification. This provision also binds employers and employees to the status quo when a union abandons the unit and fails to negotiate a new pact if the old one expires and employees fail to take action.

Other features of the law are difficult to characterize as strengths or weaknesses. Initially intended to safeguard workers' interests, these provisions contain hidden loopholes or have led to unforeseen consequences. For example:

- Excluding labor contractors from the definition of "employer." The purpose of this part of the act was to protect workers against the likelihood of a farmer canceling a contract when a crew voted for union representation. But what actually happened was that grower demand for contractors' services soared because contractors provided a shield against unionization.
- The 50 percent-of-peak employment election requirement. This provision states that elections can be held only when employment is at least fifty percent of the expected seasonal peak and ensures the migrant or part-time work force a voice in the unionization decision. Such protection comes at the expense of full-time employees who

may have different needs and preferences concerning union representation but who, by law, are part of the same bargaining unit as
seasonal and part-time workers.

- The union security clause. This feature is often hailed as a guarantee
  of a union's control over its own affairs because it gives a union dis-
  cretion in determining who is a member in good standing. But this
  provision may cede excessive control over the work force to the
  union and undermine managerial prerogatives on hiring and firing.

Perhaps the most equivocal facet of the law is its very uniqueness.
ALRA is the product of a particular historical moment in a particular state, with its confluence of personalities, issues, and events. It
reflects the industrial structure of California agriculture, which is
dominated by large commercial farms where the owners are not
necessarily the managers. The statute is embedded in a farm labor
milieu with a long history of collective and union activity and
whose constituents were strongly identified with the UFW. ALRA
also fills a void left by the NLRA's exclusion of agriculture and by
the absence of a California labor relations law that would guarantee
workers in that state the right to form unions and bargain collectively. Once California decided to take a stand on the matter of
farmworker collective bargaining, it had little choice but to enact
an agriculture-specific bill.

ALRA is a one-industry law, but for the first decade or so after its
adoption, it also seemed like a one-union law. Even though the
ALRB has certified bargaining units for more than a dozen different unions or locals since 1975, it is the UFW that has been most
closely associated with the act. Chavez and his union were so
instrumental in its development, so prominent in the farm labor
movement, and seemingly so much in control of the ALRB in its
early years that the UFW's connection with the act, in the minds of
the growers at least, was total.

At its passage, ALRA was imbued with a one-industry/one-union
aura that led to a politicization even more intense than that sur-
rounding the NLRA and its affiliated labor board. Ever since the
California act was passed, both it and the ALRB have been open to
charges of bias and partisanship. First the growers and their allies,
and then the UFW and its labor allies, charged that the law, the
rulings, the regulations, and the board staff favored one side over
the other. Under Governor Brown (1974–82), the board's alleged
pro-UFW bent infuriated farmers. The problem was exacerbated by

the apparent inability of employers and other board critics to distinguish between the UFW on the one hand, and workers and their legal rights on the other. Board actions and decisions that protected workers' rights were invariably seen as preserving the interests of the UFW. But after George Deukmejian took office, the board's alleged pro-grower tilt so alienated the UFW that it repudiated the concept of collective bargaining laws for farmworkers.

Constitutional Protections. Like California, New Jersey has no state-level labor relations law. But along with Florida, Hawaii, Missouri, New York, and Puerto Rico, New Jersey does have a constitutional provision that gives private sector employees the right to form unions and bargain collectively. Theoretically, this means employees excluded from coverage by the NLRA should be able to take advantage of their rights under the constitutional umbrella.

But acting on a constitutionally guaranteed right is another matter. New York courts have so far refused to reconcile the contradiction between the state's constitution, which guarantees farmworkers the protected right to join unions and bargain collectively, and the state's labor relations act, which denies the very same right. Although groups of affected employees have occasionally raised the issue in court, judges have rejected their constitutional challenges on the ground that employers are not obligated to bargain with workers even though workers have the right to bargain and form unions.

Courts in New Jersey, however, have taken a more activist stance. Judges have ruled that article 1, paragraph 19, of the state constitution is "self-executing," meaning it does not require enabling legislation to give it force. This holding makes the judiciary the interpreter, implementer, and enforcer of the provision. In a series of cases beginning in 1956, the state supreme court has gradually affirmed the constitutionally based organizing and bargaining rights of such diverse groups of employees as milk truck drivers, workers in nonprofit hospitals, and lay workers for religious enterprises and organizations (Goldberg and Williams 1987:744, 748, 752).

The state's farmworkers have not been overlooked. In 1971 the New Jersey Supreme Court modified the state's common law on property rights to allow lawyers, social workers, and union organizers access to farmworkers in their homes, even though they lived in camps on grower-owned property. In 1980 the court reiterated the uniqueness of the worker/grower relationship and noted the importance of legal protections for migrant farmworkers (Goldberg and Williams 1987:755, 756). Nine years later, the court specifically held that article 1, paragraph 19, of the constitution applied to farm labor.

Reliance on a constitutional provision that guarantees collective bargaining rights to farmworkers has a certain appeal. It eliminates any ambiguity about the source of these rights and clearly puts farmworkers on an equal footing with all other citizens of the state. Constitutionally based rights that rely on judicial enforcement obviate the need for potentially bruising legislative battles to secure an appropriate labor relations statute and avoid the political complications that might surround the administration of whatever law resulted.

But there are costs to relying on this approach. Depending on the courts to fill the legal void is precarious indeed. New Jersey workers who are not protected by the NLRA have no clear structure, process, or stated rules to follow, no identifiable bureaucracy to turn to, and no institutional arrangement to make theoretical rights tangible. Workers and union organizers must depend on a circuitous and painstakingly slow judicial system to guide and protect, or sometimes castigate, their activities.

The approach taken by New Jersey has had little practical effect on union organizing or collective bargaining among the state's farmworkers. Although the courts have nominally supported farmworkers' union activities, judges often insist on procedures that inhibit organizing campaigns. For example, when a judge is asked to decide whether to order a representation election, he may insist on actually seeing the workers before he concludes there is enough pro-union sentiment to warrant a vote. Labor leaders argue that this kind of procedure hurts the union: it takes time and money to physically produce each worker, and the workers may be intimidated by a court appearance. The net result is often a loss of interest in the union.

Voluntary Arrangements. The framework that defines the relationship between FLOC, cucumber and tomato growers, and food processors in northwestern Ohio and southeastern Michigan is an extralegal, ad hoc understanding. It survives because the parties are committed to making it work, not because there are legal strictures or punitive incentives.

But this unusual model, however successful it may be, has its weaknesses. For example, FLOC managed to secure a nominal agreement with Dean Foods for recognition and bargaining rights months before it won meaningful cooperation from Aunt Jane's, the Dean Foods brand that actually buys the local pickle cucumbers, and months before it obtained the necessary commitments from growers who sell to Aunt Jane's (*Crescent News* Aug. 30, 1992). FLOC has no legal standing to press the parent company, its subsidiaries, or allied growers to grant recognition despite majority support among workers for union representation. Similarly, if either the processor or growers decide to pull out of the three-way arrangement at the conclusion of a contract term, all FLOC can do is use moral suasion and the threat of consumer boycotts or organizing drives in other locales where the processor operates to bring the defector back into the fold. It has limited recourse to the law. The voluntarism of this agreement may be one of the model's virtues, but it works only so long as the tripartite relationship proves mutually beneficial.

Potentially damaging disagreements about costs associated with unionization loom on the horizon. A frequently circulated rumor suggests that Campbell may quit buying tomatoes locally and instead turn to Mexican sources. Growers and processors in North Carolina and Alabama have already adopted mechanical harvesting of pickle cucumbers, which could also replace harvesting by hand in Ohio. If FLOC demands become too steep, if growers demand too high a price from the processors, and if the processors stonewall, the entire edifice will crumble. Growers will turn to other crops or sell their land, processors will take their business elsewhere, and workers will be left without jobs. In this highly competitive and fragile industry, the limits of viability can be quickly breached.

The FLOC model has much to recommend it and some ardent advocates insist it could serve as a prototype for bargaining relationships in the farm sector. It is unlikely to be replicated elsewhere, however, because the circumstances are unusual. The arrangement involves two crops in a small area of Ohio and Michigan, and it neatly integrates the local industry structure. There are three large processors, numerous small-scale growers who have long-standing relationships with one or another of the processors, and a relatively stable and homogeneous workforce. The perseverance of Baldemar

Velasquez has been crucial to the effort, as has the leadership of several corporate officials and growers.

FLOC's strategy of getting to the growers through the processors was clever. Although other sectors of the food industry are distinguished by even tighter financial and managerial connections between grower and processor, that alone is not sufficient to ensure that a FLOC-like arrangement will evolve, let alone thrive. The set of forces and actors that propelled and defined the situation in this region probably do not exist elsewhere. The FLOC model is laudable, but is neither the best nor the only answer to the farmworkers' situation.

5. Farmworkers and the Law

Year in and year out, nature repeats itself. Time passes, seasons change, crops mature. Farmers prepare the land, map out the planting, and hope for the proper mix of rain and sun. Seeds sprout, trees blossom, fruits and vegetables ripen. As surely as the harvest comes, so do migrant and seasonal workers. They weed the fields, gather the bounty, bend and stretch and carry and drag. Year in and year out, the cycle repeats itself.

So it has been for more than a hundred years. Poorly paid and barely tolerated, farmworkers have toiled in our fields and fattened our larders. For their labors they have been sprayed with chemicals and pesticides, despised and sometimes beaten by crew leaders and deputies, and left to live in dingy shacks with unclean drinking water. Without resources, without political protection or social connections, migrant and seasonal farmworkers have somehow managed to eke out a life and a living.

Some things have changed. Technology has eliminated many of the dreariest and toughest jobs. Government regulation has attempted to restrain the worst abuses. Some employers have adopted relatively enlightened labor management practices. But there are still too many places and too many people for whom these apparent advances have little or no meaning. Farmworkers are still poor, tired, and unhealthy. They have precious few rights or protections.

History, like nature, has a tendency to repeat itself. Intense feelings of outrage and desperation have intermittently driven migrant and seasonal workers to rise up against the powerful. The

period before World War I, the Depression era, the years of the civil
rights and antiwar movements—all were interspersed with farmworker activism. Farmworkers engaged in spontaneous work stoppages and asked for small raises. They formed unions and sought
recognition and the liberty to bargain over terms and conditions of
employment. Sometimes their collective efforts to promote the
collective good led to a few improvements—a meager increase, a
nod of respect, a cupful of drinking water. But underneath even
these minor achievements, the story was always the same: either the
gains were short-lived, or the demands were ignored.

What accounts for the farmworkers' singular lack of success in
engaging in self-help through collective action? Why have unions
been unable to organize in the farm sector? The answers are many
and mutually reinforcing: fierce and bitter employer hostility toward unions; the excess supply of labor; the surging numbers of
immigrants in the work force; transience and short-term job opportunities; logistical difficulties; general indifference by mainstream
labor organizations; the absence of a strong, self-directed farmworker movement; and the lack of a legal framework for pressing
organizing rights have all hampered the evolution of farm labor
unions.

History has also shown us that *people* can make a difference. Cesar
Chavez of the UFW, along with his committed aides and determined followers, almost disproved the old maxim about the unor-
ganizability of farmworkers. Baldemar Velasquez and his supporters in FLOC are demonstrating the power of collective leverage
and the efficacies of union representation for both labor and management. In other parts of the country, leaders and movements are
inspiring farmworkers to join the struggle. At scattered sites in
California, the Northwest, and the Southwest, independent unions
and organizers are trying to forge a group consciousness and
motivate collective action. Farmworkers in Florida and the Northeast are building grass-roots organizations devoted to identifying
and meeting the social and economic needs of their fellow workers.
These groups may someday mature into labor unions seeking self-
representation in the workplace and collective bargaining with
employers.

In isolation, such organizing activities may seem insignificant.
But each time a campaign is launched and each time a worker joins
a group, a degree of fear is overcome and a certain amount of

education has occurred. Little by little, workers' feelings of empowerment may grow and leadership may emerge. Eventually migrant and seasonal workers may feel strong enough to agitate for and demand from our society the kinds of rights and protections they have long been denied. Maybe then they will pull free of the historical tide and secure the equality and equity that is their due.

Farmworkers and Labor Law Reform

If ever there were a time that augured well for reconsidering the appropriateness of organizing and collective bargaining rights for farmworkers, the mid-1990s would seem to be it. The AFL-CIO has passed resolutions calling for removal of the agricultural exemption in the NLRA. The Democrats, traditionally viewed as more sympathetic to labor issues, finally control the White House and both branches of Congress. President Bill Clinton is eager to shore up America's international competitiveness and views greater worker-management collaboration as one means of achieving that goal. In March 1993, the Department of Labor and the Department of Commerce jointly appointed a ten-member commission whose year-long task is to look beyond the NLRA and delve into the evolving realm of participatory labor-management relations. Headed by Harvard University economist John Dunlop, the Commission for the Future of Worker-Management Relations counts among its members ex-government officials with expertise in labor, union leaders, academics, and corporate executives.

What direction the commission will take, how its members will think about labor law reform and how to treat farmworkers, and how Congress and the administration will respond, remains unclear. What is woefully apparent, however, is the near-universal agreement that the NLRA and its supporting structure have failed. Employers contend that the act interferes with their ability to cultivate the kind of direct interaction with employees they insist is necessary to foster commitment and raise productivity. Labor leaders charge that employers flout the law with impunity and assert the act has ceased protecting workers' right to organize and bargain collectively. The NLRB itself is burdened by a heavy load of unfair labor practice charges, hearings, and investigations. The federal appeals courts, which enforce board rulings, are embroiled in litigation over the kind of issues that many people believe should be settled privately. Virtually everyone with any involvement in labor issues agrees the NLRA (like its California progeny, the ALRA) has been fatally politicized. Not surprisingly, each faction finds evidence to support charges that the act and the board support one side over the other.

The inherent weaknesses of the NLRA have been obvious for years. But it is only since the social contract between labor and management disintegrated in the late 1970s that a sense of urgency about the act's deficiencies emerged. The act was premised on management's acceptance of workers' right to organize and bargain collectively, on the expectation that dissident employers would be shamed and stigmatized (Edwards and Podgursky 1986:21). Once that fiction was exposed and once employers felt free to unleash a long-repressed anti-union offensive, the NLRA lost much of its force and authority.

The NLRA reflected the conviction that industrial democracy was a necessary correlate of political democracy, a principle dating to the early years of the U.S. federation (Summers 1979:29). Indeed, the act created what could be considered a constitution for industrial government: it laid out a system of law imbued with the principles of equality and procedural due process (Summers 1979:35). Although touted as a means of insuring industrial peace and the unfettered flow of interstate commerce, the NLRA's primary purpose was to promote economic progress and social justice. In its original and unamended form, the 1935 statute was decidedly partial toward freedom of association and collective bargaining (Gross 1985:10–11).

Assumptions and expectations to the contrary, intense industrial conflict raged through the end of the 1940s. Employers did not embrace the right of workers to organize and bargain collectively. They railed against a law they asserted was unbalanced in its favored treatment of labor over management. In 1947, sympathetic legislators pushed through a series of amendments to the NLRA that were supposed to equalize its handling of the adversaries. Officially known as the Labor-Management Relations Act of 1947, but commonly known as the Taft-Hartley Act after its two chief sponsors, the legislation added several provisions aimed at curbing the perceived power of organized labor. To the section creating the right to organize and bargain collectively, Taft-Hartley appended a parallel right of employees to refrain from union activity. To the section on employer unfair labor practices, Taft-Hartley added a comparable list of union unfair labor practices. What wounded the labor movement most about this latter change was that it lost the right to engage in secondary boycotts, meaning the ability to induce, encourage, force, or require anyone (employees, consumers, or other employers) to cease doing business with an employer with whom a union has a dispute.

The Taft-Hartley amendments were ostensibly intended to protect individual rights against the coercive power of employers and unions and to balance the NLRA's treatment of labor and management. What Taft-Hartley actually did, however, was to give employers an even greater tactical advantage by imposing restraints on unions' ability to organize and promote group solidarity. The amendments tilted the system against self-representation (Weiler 1990:228) and recast the government's role as promoter of collective bargaining to that of being a neutral guarantor of equal rights (Gross 1985:12).

Lack of clarity about the purpose of the act, along with its seeming contradictions, have fostered confusion in its interpretation and administration. Given that presidents generally have the opportunity to appoint a majority to the five-member board, NLRB biases seem to shift from administration to administration. Sometimes the making of precedent is subtle and evolutionary and sometimes it is dramatic and sudden. The point is, board members are molded by their own experiences and tend to follow their own philosophy in deciding cases. Their job is to provide all parties with guidance on appropriate behavior and understanding of the law. They find plenty of scope within the statute to make those judgments fit their own worldview.

During Jimmy Carter's presidency, for example, labor seemed ascendant. Employers charged that the Democratic-dominated board was writing new law, establishing new rules, and reversing decisions that were not sufficiently pro-union. One commentator, himself a former general counsel of the NLRB, contends that the board of that era was more zealous about protecting the interests of unions than about protecting the interests of individual employees (Irving 1985:397).

Such sentiment evaporated after Ronald Reagan was elected president in 1980 and installed his appointees on the board. This time, labor and its supporters charged the board was reinventing law to management's advantage. On the one hand, the board's activities during these years could be viewed as an attempt to restore the equilibrium intended by the amended NLRA. On the other hand, its actions could be construed as an effort to use administrative fiat, instead of congressional mandate, to accomplish President Reagan's ideological ends (Levy 1985:277).

The board quickly began overturning precedents set years before. Board representatives asserted they were only correcting biases that had pervaded rulings issued under more liberal regimes. They explained that the board was restoring employees' "unencumbered" right to choose or reject union representation and reinvigorating the private resolution of disputes through collective bargaining (Levy 1985:278–279). But what the board was really doing, its critics charged, was weakening organized labor and enhancing employers' power by freeing them from the constraints imposed by workers and their unions (Levy 1985:390). The NLRB seemed to be turning away from the pro-collective bargaining premise of the NLRA while aiding and abetting American employers' instinctive inclination to resist the spread of unionization.

A series of controversial decisions reinforced the widely held belief that the Reagan administration was anti-labor and pro-employer, that private property was paramount over all. Workers' right to strike and organize and management's obligation to bargain in good faith seemed irreparably compromised. The labor movement's alienation from the NLRA and the entire process grew so intense during this period that Lane Kirkland, president of the AFL-CIO, said in an August 1984 interview with the *Wall Street Journal* that union leaders might consider seeking repeal of all but the most basic rights enshrined in the original 1935 act. Even a subcommittee of the U.S. House of Representatives concluded something was amiss, when in 1984 it issued the report "Failure of Labor Law—A Betrayal of American Workers."

Dissatisfaction with the NLRA is further inflamed by its perceived conceptual shortcomings. One weakness is the act's remedial and nonpunitive cast, which focuses on in-kind reparation to victims rather than on punishment of lawbreakers. Penalties are not meant to deter but to deprive scofflaws of the advantage gained by violating the law (Townley 1986:26). The law provides for no criminal sanctions, no significant fines, and no right for employees to seek civil damages. This relatively hands-off approach may be appropriate in a society where the positive value of collective bargaining is unquestioned. Where there is neither agreement nor accommodation, as in the United States, such reserve has fostered an environment in which some employers feel free to evade and defy the law.

Employers have learned that committing unfair labor practices is often cost-effective. In their fervor to fend off any perceived union threat, many employers today actively resist union organizing drives. They fire union activists, interrogate employees about their own or others' union sympathies, threaten retaliation for supporting the union, or otherwise coerce, harass, and intimidate the work force. Although prohibited from doing these things, the chances of being caught and the penalties for being found guilty are so slight that there is little incentive to hold back. About all the board can do is order that discharged employees be reinstated with back pay (few actually return to their jobs and of those who do, most ultimately leave of their own accord), or order employers to cease and desist the unlawful behavior. Meanwhile, the employer may have derailed the organizing momentum and established how dangerous and risky supporting a union can be. A climate of fear and intimidation so permeates organizing campaigns that unions must struggle harder than ever to win bargaining rights for employees. Not only has the number of representation elections held each year dropped sharply since the early 1980s, but the union win rate has also diminished. Until 1974, unions lost fewer than half of all representation elections; since then, they have won fewer than half (BNA 1985:1).

Employers can also ignore their obligation to bargain in good faith for a first, or subsequent, contract. The NLRB cannot compel the parties to settle or become embroiled in the substance of negotiations. Surface bargaining may be an unfair labor practice but hard bargaining is not, and the thin line between the two ultimately depends on the charged party's "totality of conduct." Even if the board finds the employer has engaged in bad-faith bargaining (management has no intention of settling with the union), all the board can do is order the employer to cease and desist. Stalling, equivocating, and otherwise making a folly of negotiations has proven such a useful technique that union election victories are converted into first contracts only about 50 percent of the time (Weiler 1990:40).

Problems also arise from procedural delays built into the act. Employers, for example, have every right to challenge the board's decision on who will be included in the bargaining unit that employees seek to establish. This tactic puts off the date when employees can choose whether they want to be represented by a union. After the election, employers can also challenge the outcome and further delay the moment when they will be expected to begin negotiating a contract if the union has won. Some unfair labor practice cases tend to drag on for years as the board investigates the charges and the parties appeal the rulings. Employers often eschew early and voluntary settlements because they know that the longer the process takes, the greater the likelihood the union's support will wither or the wronged employee(s) will give up. Although forcing disputed issues through various stages of review and adjudication ensures due process (Weiler 1990:235), it comes at the price of efficiency and the abrogation of employees' rights to self-organize and bargain collectively. In many ways, the act rewards employers for their anti-union strategy.

Critics of the NLRA, notably the union movement and its allies, have argued for years that labor law reform is long overdue. The last serious attempt at repairing the NLRA was mounted during the Carter administration and involved labor leaders, representatives of the executive branch, and members of Congress. The parties crafted a bill that would have made union organizing and winning elections slightly easier and would have imposed tougher sanctions for employer unfair labor practices. But the Labor Law Reform Act of 1978 was filibustered to death. Employers wanted no part of it; not one major employer with a long-standing collective bargaining relationship rallied to its support (Summers 1979:40). Their silence provided eloquent testimony to the business community's views on the importance of industrial democracy and the worth of collective bargaining.

Reform efforts waned in the intervening years but have recently revived. The scope of proposed and potential reforms is vast. Minor changes to the NLRA could, for example, expedite the election process and limit the amount of time an employer has to influence employees' votes. Suggested structural changes would allow multi-employer bargaining units in industries with labor markets characterized by loosely defined job categories and high worker turnover (Wial 1993:672–73). Conceptual changes might require all companies larger than a certain size to establish elected employee participation committees (Weiler 1990:282). Some reformers would restore the act's original intent by removing the Taft-Hartley amendments. Others would do away with elections altogether and instead rely on signed cards indicating majority support among workers for a particular union, as is the rule in several Canadian provinces. Many would liberalize constraints on secondary boycotts, find ways to minimize administrative delays, and allow arbitration when negotiations for a first contract reach an impasse. Still others would restrict employers' now unfettered access to workers during an organizing campaign, ensure that organizers have greater access to employees, strengthen remedies and enforcement procedures, and curb the use of outside consultants. The AFL-CIO issued a working paper in 1994 detailing its objections to the current law and recommending many of the above changes.

Any of these proposals would be a boon to farmworker organizing and farm labor unions. Expedited elections or card majority, for example, would get at the problem of short-term and seasonal jobs; multi-employer bargaining units would be a way of acknowledging that farmworkers, who often have numerous employers in any given year, should be able to carry their job rights and benefits with them. For such changes to be meaningful, of course, the farmworker exclusion in the NLRA would have to be eliminated. The AFL-CIO is advocating this change, although the interest of the established farmworker unions in the act as it currently exists is muted at best. UFW leaders object to the strict prohibitions on secondary boycotts and other Taft-Hartley amendments and FLOC leaders express concern that the act makes no allowance for the kind of tripartite bargaining structure the union helped develop in the Ohio area. What stance these leaders would take on a reformulated statute clearly depends on the actual revisions.

If labor law reform is to have any value for farmworkers, and for workers in other sectors where industry and job market structure render the existing act virtually meaningless, it must move beyond the industrial model that informs the NLRA (Cobble 1990:82). Waitresses, janitors, employees of temporary services, fast-food workers, health-care workers, and garment workers isolated in cramped sweatshops are examples of employees not well served by the act. Their jobs are too fluid, places of employment too small, and wages too low for them to be able to exercise their rights as enshrined in the NLRA. Farmworkers experience many of the same organizing and bargaining challenges as other low-wage workers but for the added extra of having no legal right to organize and bargain collectively.

Certainly, farmworkers could form unions without the cover of the NLRA. They are not specifically prohibited from doing so, and farm laborers in California during the late 1960s and early 1970s and cucumber and tomato workers in Ohio more recently have proven they can indeed form unions and bargain over terms and conditions of employment without statutorily protected rights. What a law would do, however, is give farmworkers some legal protection in their struggle to unionize, lay out the guidelines for the relevant parties, and realize our espoused national value of equal treatment.

Even if Congress revises the NLRA in ways that meet the general needs of the farm labor market, the act would still need additional modifications to make it responsive to the realities of agriculture. This could be accomplished through amendments or a clear statement that the NLRB will use its rule-making authority to accommodate the special needs of agriculture. Some precedent exists for amending the act; the Labor-Management Reporting and Disclosure Act of 1959, for example, added provisions to the NLRA that make allowances for secondary boycotts in the garment industry and prehire agreements in the construction industry (an employer recognizes the union and signs a contract even before the union represents a majority of workers). A similar type of amendment reflecting the organizing challenges posed by the farm sector's distinctive structure would be useful.

Reformers should also push for a firm commitment on formal rule making. Unquestionably granted such authority under the NLRA, the board has nonetheless been reluctant to exercise its power to set definite rules that all parties can understand and follow. The board has instead chosen to view itself as a quasi-judicial agency that engages in ad hoc resolution of issues presented by the cases that come before it (Peck 1961:730). Demurrals aside, the board is really making rules through case law and bypassing the federal Administrative Procedure Act, which requires federal agencies to publish a proposed rule in the Federal Register with an effective date at least thirty days hence that invites comment from interested parties.

The virtues of such formal rule making are several. The board learns more about the issue at hand through open hearings than through the particulars of the case being considered. Although case-by-case determination allows refinements and adjustments to board policy, such fine tuning is haphazard and dependent on which parties have the resources and persistence to pursue a given case (Bernstein 1970:588, 591). Rule making also insulates the board against charges of arbitrariness and capriciousness (Peck 1961:746) and leads to clear enunciation of policy, uniform treatment, certainty, and minimal confusion on the part of labor and management. It also reduces litigation costs and frees the board to spend more time on cases that truly merit careful balancing (Subrin 1981:109).

Despite the recognized advantages of rule making, only once has the board used its authority to establish a substantive rule. After years of litigation over the determination of bargaining units in acute-care hospitals, in 1987 the board finally announced rules that set the occupational boundaries for these units. The board held hearings, revised its proposal, fought the case in federal court against the American Hospital Association, and finally won vindication in 1991 with a 9–0 ruling by the Supreme Court. Some observers hope this experience will inspire the board to use its rule-making authority more habitually and that President Clinton will appoint members who aggressively invoke this power.

The board's exercise of its rule-making authority would be crucial to farmworkers. The shortness of the season, the transience of the workforce, the growing reliance on labor contractors, the large number of undocumented workers, the small size of most farms, the concentration of large commercial farms in several regions, and farmers' relationship with processors and retailers are just some of the particular characteristics of agriculture that argue for special accommodation under the NLRA or whatever may issue from it. Farmworkers, their advocates, and their allies need to be certain that these peculiarities will be recognized before they urge any change in the exclusionary language of the NLRA. Waiting for case law to recognize critical distinctions is risky, expensive, and takes far too long. A commitment to rule making and special amendments are the keys to making the NLRA a viable statute for farmworkers. Further reform of the statute along the lines noted above would also solidify its value for migrant and seasonal farmworkers.

The Case for Farmworker Unions

Labor unions have always occupied an uneasy perch in American society. Employers complain that unions impinge on their managerial prerogatives, stand in the way of efficiency, cut into profits, and bring an unwelcome tone of adversarialism and legalism to the workplace. Economists allege that unions distort the allocation of resources by driving up wages in unionized companies and pushing excess workers into the unorganized sector of the economy, which in turn lowers wages for those lucky enough to even find jobs. Some union critics charge that labor organizations are elitist and inward looking, caring only about amassing power for the leadership, enriching the lives of their members, and protecting incompetent workers at the expense of the young and minorities. And some people simply assert that unions and self-organization contradict the ideals of individual initiative and opportunity upon which this country was founded.

Yet many observers laud the contributions unions have made to American society. Some employers concede that the presence of a union means stability and lower turnover, higher skill levels, and better managerial practices. Some economists dare to suggest that unions lead to higher productivity, better information flows to management, strong employee morale, and reduced income disparities. Many ordinary citizens commend the union movement for its commitment to protecting workers against arbitrary treatment, for helping to settle problems and grievances, for negotiating minimum guarantees, for promoting employee participation, and for being an outpost of democracy in the workplace. Organized labor is also credited with pursuing a legislative agenda that enhances our social and environmental welfare in such areas as health and safety, unemployment insurance, and legal aid to the poor.

This duality of attitudes toward unions makes them the focus of much controversy and shrill emotion. Academics Richard Freeman and James Medoff, in their classic volume *What Do Unions Do?* (1984), describe and test at length the monopoly face and voice/response face of American unions. Not surprisingly, they conclude that unions manifest both faces. On the positive side, unions raise wages, minimize income inequality, reduce turnover, promote better training and skill retention, boost productivity, tighten standards and accountability, posit explicit rules, and reinforce our economic and political freedoms.

But unions also exact a price. They may prompt managers to make less than ideal decisions about hiring and investment, and they sometimes lead to strikes that reduce the gross national product. Unions are also associated with work rules that may impair a company's ability to respond to changing technology and market conditions, high wages at the expense of nonunion workers in other sectors of the economy, and lower levels of profitability. What unions ultimately do, say Freeman and Medoff, depends on the industry and its degree of concentration, on management actions, on union actions, and on what both sides do together (Freeman and Medoff 1984:177, 185).

American unions are caught in a bind. They show up on the positive side of the social balance sheet but on the negative side of the corporate balance sheet (Freeman and Medoff 1984:248). The public seems to support the voice/response face but expresses hostility toward the monopoly face. The problem is Americans believe the monopoly face is dominant. During the forty-five years following passage of the NLRA, public opinion of unions declined dramatically (BNA 1985:1, 10). Although a 1988 Gallup Poll shows that public opinion has rebounded (Weiler 1990:298), the challenge still confronting unions is how to enhance the voice/response face and soften the monopoly face.

Unions suffered a string of stunning setbacks during the 1980s. The social contract linking labor and management in a relatively amicable and practical accord crumbled under the weight of intense international competition and the burden of surging individual rights. Heavy manufacturing, the core of labor's constituency, lost hundreds of thousands of jobs. Economic growth slowed, productivity drooped, and corporate profits declined. Unions seemed stuck in a mold of defending their turf against encroachments from the outside and were ill-equipped to suggest creative solutions to the nation's economic malaise. Sensing labor's vulnerability, employers dropped all pretense of seeking rapport with their unions and went on the offensive, demanding concessions and fighting unions at every pass. The number of unfair labor practice charges levied against employers surged and union election victories plummeted. Even the federal labor board seemed unsympathetic to labor's plight. During much of that era, the NLRB was dominated by Republican stalwarts and an outspokenly anti-union chairman.

The 1990s may prove to be a more auspicious decade for the labor movement. A Democratic president was elected in 1992 and the new administration seems interested in repairing the frayed relations that existed between labor and the federal government under the presidencies of Ronald Reagan and George Bush. Unions themselves are eager to sign up new members and are beginning to think beyond the obvious pool of high-wage, high-skill industrial workers. A few of the more progressive unions, such as the Service Employees' International Union (SEIU) and the International Ladies' Garment Workers' Union (ILGWU), are casting about for creative ways to reach the millions of unorganized low-wage, low-skill workers in countless industrial sweatshops and in the burgeoning service sector of the economy. Increasingly, the public seems to be rooting for their success.

This is all to the good. Unions are, or at least ought to be, an indelible part of our social, political, and economic fabric. Work is such a central component of our lives, providing us with our means of support and demanding of our psychic and physical energies, that it requires certain considerations. In a democratic society where citizens are free to express their opinions, elect representatives, and pursue their own inclinations, two fundamental questions arise: Who represents employees and their interests in the workplace? And what form will that representation take? (Weiler 1990:3–6)

Labor unions and the corresponding system of collective bargaining provide one obvious answer. Unions protect individuals against the vagaries and prejudices of an imperfectly competitive labor market, restrain the arbitrary impulses of managerial authority, and channel information from the shop floor to the executive suite. They provide employees with collective leverage against powerful employers. And they connote dignity, respect, and fairness. The process and structure of collective bargaining discharges these functions and serves as a governance mechanism for employees' protection and participation (Weiler 1990:8).

Although alternatives to collective bargaining exist, they are not as effective. The "market," which theoretically balances the supply of and demand for labor through adjustments in wages, benefits, and working conditions, ignores the fact that employers have signif-

icantly more market power than do individuals. Government regulation, which fills in cracks left by the "imperfect market," sets
minimum standards and passes laws pertaining to such matters as
health and safety and retirement guarantees. But the government's
enforcement record is spotty, related litigation is costly and time
consuming, and workers are often unaware of the rules or what they
should do to enforce their rights. Another alternative, direct employee participation, has become increasingly popular among nonunion and unionized companies alike. In this approach, managers
foster commitment and open communication through a variety of
techniques, including work teams and problem-solving task forces.
But this is a scheme of participation without protection, because at
any time employers can shut the program down, ignore suggestions,
fire outspoken workers, and manage however they see fit (Weiler
1990:17–33).

Unions are by no means model institutions, but they are the best
we have. Unions are indispensable to a complex industrial society
that adheres to democratic norms. While they may induce dislocations and inefficiencies in an ideal system, they compensate for the
routine and mundane failings of our very real political, economic,
and social system. Unions can help broker an equitable distribution
of resources and rewards, serve as advocates for individuals and
groups of workers, provide a bulwark against fear in the workplace,
and promote egalitarian values.

No rational reason exists to deny farmworkers the benefits that
attach to a vital union movement. The rights of seasonal workers in
many industries, such as resort and construction, are not disputed
and clearly guaranteed by the NLRA. The seasonal character of the
farm labor force and the unpredictable nature of farming cannot
justify agriculture's exemption from the act, or its special treatment
by other pieces of protective labor legislation. Farmers' propensity
to transfer much of the uncertainty onto a vulnerable work force
and the miserable conditions most farmworkers endure are strong
arguments for inclusion in our collective bargaining statute. The
transience, heterogeneity, and purported ambivalence of farmworkers toward unions are simply lame excuses that have nothing to
do with the matter of rights and equal protection under the law.

To state the case in slightly different terms, moral and ethical
claims to fairness, justice, and equity ought to suffice as reasons for
bringing farmworkers under the scope of the NLRA. If farm labor

unions and collective bargaining also improve morale, raise productivity, and induce more efficient management techniques, all
the better. Farm prosperity is no doubt important. So too is the
quality of life, in all its manifold meanings, for the thousands of
men, women, and children who take their livelihood from the land.
It is these intangibles, the elusive outcomes that speak so eloquently
about the character of our society, that are truly compelling.

References

AFL-CIO Committee on the Evolution of Work. 1985. "The Changing Situation of Workers and their Unions." February.

AFL-CIO, Industrial Union Department. 1994. "Workplace Rights: Democracy on the Job."

Agricultural Labor Relations Board (ALRB). 1976–1992. Annual reports.

Auerbach, Jerold S. 1966. *Labor and Liberty: The La Follette Committee and the New Deal.* Indianapolis: Bobbs-Merrill.

Barr, Donald J., Aurora Demarco, Carl Henry Feuer, Robin Lee Whittlesey. 1988. "Liberalism to the Test: African-American Migrant Farmworkers and the State of New York." Institute Document #88-2, SUNY/New York State African-American Institute. February.

Barry, D. Marshall. 1989. The Adverse Impact of Immigration on Florida's Farmworkers. Center for Labor Research and Studies, Florida International University, Gainesville.

Bernstein, Merton C. 1970. "The NLRB's Adjudication–Rule Making Dilemma under the Administrative Procedure Act." *Yale Law Journal* 79 (March):571–622.

Bok, Derek C. 1971. "The Distinctive Character of American Labor Law." *Harvard Law Review* 84 (April):1394–1463.

Bonilla-Santiago, Gloria. 1988. *Organizing Puerto Rican Migrant Farmworkers: The Experience of Puerto Ricans in New Jersey.* New York: Peter Lang.

BNA. 1985. "Unions Today: New Tactics to Tackle Tough Times." Washington, D.C.: BNA.

Chi, Peter S.K. 1986. "Employment and Economic Profiles of Black Migrant Farmworkers in New York and Implications for Future Immigration Policy." Paper presented at the annual meeting of the Rural Sociological Society, Salt Lake City, Utah, August 26–30.

———. 1989. "A Tale of Two Homes: A Study of Housing Conditions of Migrant Farmworkers." Paper presented at the fifth annual conference on the Sociology of Housing, St. Paul, Minn., November 19.

Cobble, Dorothy Sue. 1990. "Union Strategies for Organizing and Representing the New Service Workforce." In *Proceedings of the Forty-third Annual Meeting, Industrial Relations Research Association*, 76–84. Madison, Wis.: IRRA.

Cockcroft, James D. 1986. *Outlaws in the Promised Land*. New York: Grove Press.

Commission on Agricultural Workers. 1992. *Report of the Commission on Agricultural Workers*. Washington, D.C.: GPO.

Commission on Security and Cooperation in Europe. 1993. *Migrant Farmworkers in the United States: Implementation of the Helsinki Accords, Briefings*. Washington, D.C. May.

Cottle, Rex L., Hugh H. Macaulay, and Bruce Yandle. 1983. "Some Economic Effects of the California Agricultural Labor Relations Act." *Journal of Labor Research* 4 (Fall):315–24.

Craddock, Brian R., ed. 1988. *Federal and State Employment Standards and U.S. Farm Labor: A Reference Guide to Labor Protective Laws and Their Applicability in the Agricultural Workplace*. Austin, Texas: Motivation Education and Training.

Dingfelder, John J. 1989. "The 1983 Migrant and Seasonal Agricultural Workers Act Results in a Harvest of Litigation." *Journal of Agricultural Taxation and Law* 11 (Spring):3–29.

Duffield, James A., Mitchell J. Morehart, and Robert Coltrane. 1989. "Labor Expenditures Help Determine Farms Affected by Immigration Reform." Agricultural Information Bulletin No. 557, U.S. Department of Agriculture, Economic Research Division. April.

Edwards, Richard, and Michael Podgursky. 1986. "The Unraveling Accord: American Unions in Crisis." In *Unions in Crisis and Beyond*, edited by Richard Edwards, Paolo Garonna, and Franz Tödtling, 14–60. Dover, Mass.: Auburn House.

Feldacker, Bruce. *Labor Guide to Labor Law*. 1990. Englewood Cliffs, N.J.: Prentice Hall.

Fisher, Lloyd H. 1953. *The Harvest Labor Market in California*. Cambridge, Mass.: Harvard University Press.

Fogel, Walter, ed. 1985. *California Farm Labor Relations and Law*. Monograph and Research Series, no. 41. Los Angeles: Institute of Industrial Relations, University of California.

———, ed. 1989. *Application of the Makewhole Remedy Under California's Agricultural Labor Relations Act: Litigious Refusals to Bargain*. Monograph and Research Series, no. 50. Los Angeles: Institute of Industrial Relations, University of California.

Foner, Philip S. 1984. *First Facts of American Labor*. New York: Holmes & Meier.

Freeman, Richard B., and James L. Medoff. 1984. *What Do Unions Do?* New York: Basic Books.

Friedland, William H., Amy E. Barton, and Robert J. Thomas. 1981. *Manufacturing Green Gold*. Cambridge: Cambridge University Press.

Fuller, Varden. 1955. *Labor Relations in Agriculture*. Berkeley: Institute of Industrial Relations, University of California.

————. 1991. *Hired Hands in California's Farm Fields: Collected Essays on California's Farm Labor History and Policy*. Giannini Foundation Special Report, University of California.

Fuller, Varden, and John W. Mamer. 1978. "Constraints on California Farm Worker Unionization." *Industrial Relations* 17 (May):143–55.

Galarza, Ernesto. 1964. *Merchants of Labor: The Mexican Bracero Story*. Charlotte, N.C.: McNally & Loftin.

Glass, Judith Chanin. 1968. "Organization in Salinas." *Monthly Labor Review* 91 (June):24–27.

Goldberg, Richard A., and Robert F. Williams. 1987. "Farmworkers' Organizational and Collective Bargaining Rights in New Jersey: Implementing Self-Executing State Constitutional Rights." *Rutgers Law Journal* 18 (Summer):729–63.

Grodin, Joseph H. 1976. "California Agricultural Labor Act: Early Experience." *Industrial Relations* 15 (October):275–94.

Gross, James A. 1985. "Conflicting Statutory Purposes: Another Look at Fifty Years of NLRB Law Making." *Industrial and Labor Relations Review* 39 (October):7–18.

Grubbs, Donald H. 1971. *Cry from the Cotton: The Southern Tenant Farmers' Union and the New Deal*. Chapel Hill: University of North Carolina Press.

Harrington, Michael. 1964. *The Other America: Poverty in the United States*. New York: Macmillan.

Harrison, Bennett, and Barry Bluestone. 1988. *The Great U-Turn: Corporate Restructuring and the Polarizing of America*. New York: Basic Books.

Hartmire, Chris. 1978. "UFW: Pushing Ahead in a New Day." *Fellowship* (September):11–13.

Hastings, Janice E. 1990. "1989 Dairy Farm Summary." Farm Credit Banks of Springfield, Mass. April.

Heppel, Monica. 1990. "The Apple Industry in Wayne County, New York." In *Immigration Reform and Perishable Crop Agriculture: Case Studies*, vol. 2, edited by Sandra L. Amendola and Monica L. Heppel, 75–79. Washington, D.C.: Center for Immigration Studies.

Hermanson, Jeff. 1993. "Organizing for Justice." *Labor Research Review* 20:53–62.

Holt, James S. 1984. "Introduction to the Seasonal Farm Labor Problem." In *Seasonal Agricultural Labor Markets in the United States*, edited by Robert D. Emerson. Ames, Iowa: Iowa State University Press.

Interagency Workgroup on Migrant Health Care. 1987. *Statewide Strategies for Health Care for Migrant and Seasonal Farmworkers*. Report prepared for the New York State Department of Health, Division of Planning, Policy, and Resource Development. December.

Irving, John S. 1985. " 'Failure' of the Labor Laws: An Election Year Issue." *Capital University Law Review* 14 (Spring):387–402.

Jamieson, Stuart. (1945), 1976. *Labor Unionism in American Agriculture*. U.S. Government Printing Office, Bulletin No. 836. Reprint. New York: Arno Press.

Jenkins, J. Craig. 1985. *The Politics of Insurgency: The Farm Worker Movement in the 1960s*. New York: Columbia University Press.

————, and Charles Perrow. 1977. "Insurgency of the Powerless: Farm Worker Movements, 1946–1972." *American Sociological Review* 42 (April):249–67.

Kenny, John J. 1986. *Primer of Labor Relations*. Washington, D.C.: Bureau of National Affairs.

Kissam, Ed, and David Griffith. 1991. *The Farm Labor Supply Study: 1989–1990*. Berkeley: Micro Methods.

Koziara, Karen S. 1968. "Collective Bargaining on the Farm." *Monthly Labor Review* 91 (June):3–9.

————. 1980. "Agriculture." In *Collective Bargaining: Contemporary American Experience*, edited by Gerald G. Somers, 263–314. Madison, Wis.: Industrial Relations Research Association.

Kuttner, Robert. 1984. *The Economic Illusion: False Choices between Prosperity and Social Justice*. Boston: Houghton Mifflin.

Leggett, John C. 1991. *Mining the Fields*. Highland Park, N.J.: Raritan Institute.

Levy, Herman M. 1976. "The Agricultural Labor Relations Act of 1975—La Esperanza de California Para El Futuro." *Santa Clara Lawyer* 15:783–816.

Levy, Paul Alan. 1985. "The Unidimensional Perspective of the Reagan Labor Board." *Rutgers Law Journal* 16 (Winter):269–390.

Lewin, Jeff L. 1976. "Representatives of Their Own Choosing: Practical Considerations in the Selection of Bargaining Representatives for Seasonal Farmworkers." *California Law Review* 64 (May):732–94.

Lloyd, Jack, Philip Martin, and John Mamer. 1988. "The Ventura Citrus Labor Market." Giannini Information Series No. 88-1, Division of Agriculture and Natural Resources, Giannini Foundation of Agricultural Economics, University of California, Oakland. April.

London, Joan, and Henry Anderson. 1970. *So Shall Ye Reap*. New York: Thomas Y. Crowell.

McWilliams, Carey. (1935, 1939), 1971. *Factories in the Field*. Reprint. Salt Lake City: Peregrine Publishers.

Majka, Linda C., and Theo J. Majka. 1982. *Farm Workers, Agribusiness, and the State*. Philadelphia: Temple University Press.

Maloney, Thomas R., and Sue A. Woodruff. 1989. "Wages and Benefits of Full Time Non Family Employees on Larger than Average New York State Dairy Farms." A.E. Res. 89-20, Department of Agricultural Economics, Cornell University Agricultural Experiment Station, New York State College of Agriculture and Life Sciences, Cornell University.

Mamer, John W., and Donald Rosedale. 1981. "The Management of Seasonal Farm Workers under Collective Bargaining." Leaflet 21147, Division of Agricultural Sciences, University of California, Davis.

Marshall, Ray. 1987. *Unheard Voices: Labor and Economic Policy in a Competitive World*. New York: Basic Books.

Martin, Philip L. 1983. "A Comparison of California's ALRA and the Federal NLRA." *California Agriculture* (July–August):6–8.

———. 1985. *Seasonal Workers in American Agriculture: Background and Issues*. Washington, D.C.: National Commission for Employment Policy.

———. 1986. "Western Farm Labor Issues." *Contemporary Policy Issues* 4 (January):72–86.

———. 1987. "California's Farm Labor Market." No. 87-1. Agricultural Issues Center, University of California, Davis.

———, Suzanne Vaupel, and Daniel L. Egan. 1988. *Unfulfilled Promise: Collective Bargaining in California Agriculture*. Boulder, Colo.: Westview Press.

———. 1990a. "Harvest of Confusion: Immigration Reform and California Agriculture." *International Migration Review* 24 (Spring):69–95.

———. 1990b. "The Outlook for Agricultural Labor in the 1990s." *Davis Law Review* 23 (Spring):499–523.

Meister, Dick, and Anne Loftis. 1977. *A Long Time Coming: The Struggle to Unionize America's Farm Workers*. New York: Macmillan.

Mines, Richard, and Philip L. Martin. 1986. "A Profile of California Farmworkers." Giannini Information Series No. 86-2, University of California.

Mines, Richard, Susan Gabbard, and Ruth Samardick. 1992. "U.S. Farmworkers in the Post-IRCA Period." In *Report of the Commission on Agricultural Workers*, Appendix 1, 635–700.

Mitchell, H. L. 1979. *Mean Things Happening in This Land*. Montclair, N.J.: Allenheld, Osmun & Co.

Mitchell, Stuart J., III. 1981. "Farmwork and Farmworkers in New York State." In *Prepare*, a publication of the New York State Council of Churches (September).

Moore, Truman E. 1965. *The Slaves We Rent*. New York: Random House.

Morin, Alexander. 1952. *The Organizability of Farm Labor in the U.S.* Cambridge: Harvard University Press.

Nelkin, Dorothy. 1970. *On the Season: Aspects of the Migrant Labor System.* Ithaca, N.Y.: New York State School of Industrial and Labor Relations.

New York Agricultural Statistics Service. 1990. *New York Agricultural Statistics 1989–1990.* Albany: New York State Department of Agriculture and Markets, Division of Statistics.

Peck, Cornelius J. 1961. "The Atrophied Rule-Making Powers of the National Labor Relations Board." *Yale Law Journal* 70 (April):695–761.

Polopolus, Leo C. 1989. "Agricultural Labor in the 1990s." Staff Paper no. 367. Food and Resource Economics Department, Institute of Food and Agricultural Sciences, University of Florida, Gainesville. September.

Polopolus, Leo C., Sharon Moon, and Noy Chunkasut. 1989. "Farm Labor in the Florida Fruit, Vegetable, and Ornamental Industries." Working paper, Department of Food and Resource Economics, Florida Cooperative Extension Service, Institute of Food and Agricultural Sciences, University of Florida, Gainsville.

Ray, Douglas E. 1987. "The 1986–1987 Labor Board: Has the Pendulum Slowed?" *Boston College Law Review* 29 (December):1–20.

Rochin, Refugio I. 1977. "New Perspectives on Agricultural Labor Relations in California." *Labor Law Journal* 28 (July):395–402.

Rosenberg, Howard R. 1987. "Getting Work Done: Labor Issues in the Food and Fiber System." In *The Farm and Food System in Transition—Emerging Policy Issues.* East Lansing: Cooperative Extension Service, Michigan State University.

Rosenberg, Howard R., Roger E. Garrett, Ronald E. Voss, David L. Mitchell. 1990. "Labor and Competitive Agricultural Technology in 2010." In *Agriculture in California on the Brink of a New Millennium,* edited by Harold O. Carter and Carole F. Nuckton. Davis: University of California Agricultural Issues Center.

Rural Realignment Project. 1989. "New Thinking for California Agriculture: A Discussion Paper on Farm Worker and Family Farmer Relations." Berkeley: Family Farm Organizing Resource Center. December.

Sanchez, Guadalupe L., and Jesus Romo. 1981. "Organizing Mexican Undocumented Farm Workers on Both Sides of the Border." San Diego: Program in United States-Mexican Studies, University of California.

Schwartz, Harry. 1945. *Seasonal Farm Labor in the United States.* New York: Columbia University Press.

Segur, W. H., and Varden Fuller. 1976. "California's Farm Labor Elections: An Analysis of the Initial Results." *Monthly Labor Review* 99 (December):25–30.

Slichter, Sumner H., James J. Healy, and E. Robert Livernash. 1960. *The Impact of Collective Bargaining on Management.* Washington, D.C.: Brookings Institution.

Stanton, B., W. Knoblauch, and L. Putnam. 1989. *Census of Agricultural Highlights: New York State 1987.* A.E. Ext. 89-38. Department of Agricultural Economics, New York State College of Agriculture and Life Sciences, Cornell University, Ithaca, N.Y. November.

Stein, Walter J. 1973. *California and the Dust Bowl Migration.* Westport, Conn.: Greenwood Press.

Subrin, Berton B. 1981. "Conserving Energy at the Labor Board: The Case for Making Rules on Collective Bargaining Units." *Labor Law Journal* 32 (February):105–13.

Summers, Clyde W. 1979. "Industrial Democracy: America's Unfulfilled Promise." *Cleveland State Law Review* 28:29–49.

Task Force on Agricultural Employment, Education, and Labor. 1990. *Report of the Governor's Task Force on Agricultural Employment, Education and Labor.* Albany: New York State Commissions Department.

Terry, Jim. 1983. "Campbell Soup in Hot Water with Organized Labor." *Business and Society Review* (Summer):37–41.

Townley, Barbara. 1986. *Labor Law Reform in U.S. Industrial Relations.* Aldershot, England: Gower.

U.S. Bureau of the Census. 1988. *1987 Census of Agriculture.* Prepared by the Bureau of the Census, Washington, D.C.

U.S. General Accounting Office. 1989. "Immigration Reform: Potential Impact on West Coast Farm Labor." HRD-89-89. Washington, D.C. August.

———. 1988. "The H-2A Program: Protections for U.S. Farmworkers." PEMD-89-3. Washington, D.C. October.

Weiler, Paul. 1983. "Promises to Keep: Securing Workers' Rights to Self-Organization Under the NLRA." *Harvard Law Review* 96 (June): 1769–1827.

———. 1986. "Milestone or Tombstone: The Wagner Act at Fifty." *Harvard Journal on Legislation* 23 (Winter):1–31.

———. 1990. *Governing the Workplace: The Future of Labor and Employment Law.* Cambridge: Harvard University Press.

Wells, Miriam J., and Martha S. West. 1989. "Regulation of the Farm Labor Market: An Assessment of Farm Worker Protections Under California's Agricultural Labor Relations Act." Working paper no. 5, Working Group on Farm Labor and Rural Poverty, California Institute for Rural Studies, Davis. February.

White, Harold C. 1973. "The Labor Unions in the Fields: The Arizona Farm Labor Law." *Arizona Business* 31 (October): 17–36.

———, and William Gibney. 1980. "The Arizona Farm Labor Law: A Supreme Court Test." *Labor Law Journal* 31 (February):87–99.

Wial, Howard. 1993. "The Emerging Organizational Structure of Unionism in Low-Wage Services." *Rutgers Law Review* 45 (Spring):671–738.

Yates, Michael D. 1978. "The 'Make Whole' Remedy for Employer Refusal to Bargain: Early Experience Under the California Agricultural Labor Relations Act." *Labor Law Journal* 29 (October):666–76.

Interviews

California Interviews

Angstadt, H. Edwin. President, Grower/Shipper Vegetable Association of Central California. 8/10/90.

Bennett, Don. Consultant and executive director, Agricultural Personnel Management Associates. 8/8/90.

Berman, Howard. U.S. congressman and former California state assemblyman. 7/9/90.

Brenner, Marvin J. Assistant general counsel, Agricultural Labor Relations Board. 8/29/90.

Brown, Gerald. Former chair, Agricultural Labor Relations Board. 8/28/90.

Burciaga, David. Former director of negotiations, United Farm Workers. 8/10/90.

Church, Andrew. Attorney, Abramson, Church & Stave. 8/29/90.

Cohen, Jerry. Former chief counsel, United Farm Workers. 8/26/90.

De Leon, Ralph. President, Servicios Agricolas Mexicanos. 8/30/90.

Drake, Jim. Former staff member, United Farm Workers. 6/26/90.

Dresser, Robert S. Board counsel, Agricultural Labor Relations Board. 8/27/90 and 1/7/91.

Fogel, Walter. Professor, Graduate School of Management, University of California, Los Angeles. 9/11/90.

Gabriel, Roy. Director of labor affairs, California Farm Bureau. 8/27/90.

Guilin, Alfonso A. Executive vice president, Limoneira Associates. 8/30/90.

Titles and affiliations may now differ; this listing reflects positions at the time of the interview. The list is not inclusive; some people chose to speak strictly off the record.

Haller, Thomas. Executive secretary, California Association of Family Farmers. 8/28/90.

Henning, Patrick W. Chief consultant, Assembly Committee on Labor and Employment. 8/28/90.

Hernandez, Manuel. Senior consultant to California Senate Toxic and Public Safety Management Committee and assistant to Senator Art Torres. 8/8/90.

Hershenbaum, Irv. National representative, United Farm Workers. 6/28/90.

Johnston, Mike. Business representative, Teamsters Local 890. 8/29/90.

Lloyd, Jack. Agricultural labor specialist and former general manager, Coastal Growers Association. 8/31/90.

McCarthy, John. Former member, Agricultural Labor Relations Board. 9/24/90.

Majka, Linda. Associate professor, Department of Sociology and Anthropology, University of Dayton. 6/25/90.

Majka, Theo. Associate professor, Department of Sociology and Anthropology, University of Dayton. 6/25/90.

Martin, Philip L. Professor, Department of Agricultural Economics, University of California, Davis. 6/22/90 and 9/10/90.

Matoian, Richard. Director, government relations, California Grape and Tree Fruit League. 8/20/90.

Maturino, Pete. President, Independent Union of Agricultural Workers. 8/10/90.

Meneken, Cliff. Attorney, Agricultural Labor Relations Board. 9/5/90.

Moore, Barbara. Administrative law judge, Agricultural Labor Relations Board. 7/9/90.

Quandt, Richard. President and general counsel, Grower/Shipper Vegetable Association (Santa Barbara and San Luis Obispo Counties). 8/30/90.

Rochin, Refugio I. Professor, Department of Agricultural Economics, University of California, Davis. 8/28/90.

Rosenberg, Howard. Cooperative extension specialist, Department of Agricultural and Resource Economics, University of California, Berkeley. 6/27/90.

Roy, Robert A. President and general counsel, Ventura County Agricultural Association. 8/30/90.

Runsten, Dave. Director of research, Working Group on Farm Labor and Rural Poverty, California Institute for Rural Studies. 6/28/90.

Smith, Roger. Former staff member, Agricultural Labor Relations Board. 9/7/90.

Sobel, Thomas. Administrative law judge, Agricultural Labor Relations Board. 9/25/90.

Trevinio, Shirley. Field examiner, Agricultural Labor Relations Board. 9/5/90.

Vaupel, Suzanne. Agricultural economist. 6/14/90.

Villarejo, Don. Executive director, California Institute for Rural Studies. 7/5/90 and 2/6/91.

Williams, Russell L. President, Agricultural Producers. 8/9/90.

Young, Casey. Consultant, California Senate Industrial Relations Committee. 8/27/90.

New York Interviews

Bailey, Charles, Jr. Farmer. 10/5/90.

Bane, Norman W. Personnel manager, Comstock Michigan Fruit Division. 9/14/90.

Barber, Roger. Farmer and member of New York State Farm Minimum Wage Advisory Council. 9/10/90.

Bennett, Howard "Whitey." President, Teamsters Local 294 and vice president, New York State AFL-CIO. 9/17/90.

Blake, Marshall. President, Service Employees' International Union Local 200A. 10/29/90.

Brown, Hezekiah. Chairman, New York State Mediation Service. 9/17/90.

Cavallaro, John. Farmer. 10/11/90.

Cavallaro, Sam. Farmer. 10/11/90.

Cole, Pandora. Staff member, Cornell Migrant Program, Cornell Cooperative Extension. 9/13/90.

Couch, James. Assistant deputy county executive, Suffolk County. 9/5/90.

Crist, Joy. Farmer. 9/5/90.

DeMay, Clifford J. Owner, DeMay Labor. 9/13/90.

Dietrich, Robert. Rural employment supervisor, New York State Department of Labor. 6/29/90.

Dodge, David M. Special assistant to the commissioner, New York State Department of Agriculture and Markets. 8/6/90.

Dressel, Rod. Farmer. 10/16/90.

Dressel, Rod, Jr. Farmer. 10/16/90.

Embry, Kay. Extension associate, Cornell Migrant Program, Cornell Cooperative Extension. 6/4/90.

Fitch, Gary. Farmer and member of New York State Farm Minimum Wage Advisory Council. 10/9/90.

Funiciello, John. Chairman, Solidarity Committee of the Capitol District and staff member, AFSCME. 9/5/90 and 10/22/90.

Furber, Sheldon. Farmer. 10/5/90.

Gonzales, Laura. Program assistant, Interagency Coordinating Committee on Farmworker Services. 9/27/90.

Haley, Thomas. Assistant to president, New York State AFL-CIO. 8/7/90.

Harnett, Thomas. Former attorney, Farmworker Legal Services of New York. 7/9/90.

Hardie, David E. Dairy farmer. 10/22/90.

Hearn, Dave. Staff member, Rural Opportunities, Inc. 8/9/90.

Helmich, Helen. Farmer. 9/12/90.

Henehan, Brian. Extension associate, College of Agriculture and Life Sciences, Cornell University. 9/26/90.

Hernandez, Jorge. Former farmworker. 8/15/90.

Hooker, Patrick. Associate director, government relations, New York Farm Bureau. 8/6/90.

Horwitz, Charles. Senior attorney, New York State Department of Labor. 6/13/90, 8/17/90, 6/28/93.

Howland, Robert. Dairy farmer. 7/13/90.

Huerta, Dolores. First vice president, United Farm Workers of America. 10/9/90.

Irwin, Donald. Senior rural employment representative. New York State Department of Labor. 7/12/90.

Johnston, Edward. Milk marketing specialist, New York State Department of Agriculture and Markets. 6/13/90.

Joyce, John. President, Wayne County chapter NAACP and former staff member, Cornell Migrant Program, Cornell Cooperative Extension. 9/13/90.

Keeney-Mulligan, Rev. Gail. Mid-Hudson Catskill Rural/Migrant Ministry. 9/12/90.

Laufman, Barbara. Director, New York State District, International Ladies' Garment Workers' Union. 9/17/90.

Lauzon, David. Rural employment representative, New York State Department of Labor. 6/29/90.

Low, Diego. Student. 10/17/90 and 1/29/91.

Lynch, Robert. Director, BOCES Geneseo Migrant Center. 7/16/90.

Maloney, Thomas. Extension associate, College of Agriculture and Life Sciences, Cornell University. 6/15/90.

Manuel, Freddy. Member, New York State Farm Minimum Wage Advisory Council. 9/17/90.

Milligan, Robert A. Professor, Department of Agricultural Economics. College of Agriculture and Life Sciences, Cornell University. 6/8/90.

Mitchell, Al. Farmer. 10/5/90.

Mitchell, Stuart J., III. Executive director, Rural Opportunities, Inc., and member, New York State Farm Minimum Wage Advisory Council. 6/29/90.

Mooney, James F. Farm labor specialist, Wage and Hour Division, U.S. Department of Labor. 8/1/90.

Morris, Deborah. Rural labor service representative, New York State Department of Labor. 9/12/90.

Myers, Roy A. Executive vice president, Curtice Burns Foods and member, New York State Farm Minimum Wage Advisory Council. 9/14/90.

Nadeau, Donald. Director of procurement, fruits and concentrates, Cadbury Beverages, Inc. 10/2/90.

Naeye, Don. Farmer. 10/5/90.

O'Connor, Joseph D. Farm labor specialist, Wage and Hour Division, U.S. Department of Labor. 7/6/90.

Orbaker, Gary. Farmer. 10/5/90.

Peck, Marvin. President, New England Apple Council. 9/17/90.

Pollard, Ken. Executive officer, Western New York Apple Growers. 8/23/90.

Polsinello, Richard J. Director of labor standards, New York State Department of Labor. 8/7/90.

Rau, Carmen. Attorney, Institute for Farmworker Justice. 10/17/90.

Russo, Joe. Farmer and executive vice president, Valley Growers Coop. 7/9/90 and 10/16/90.

Schmidt, James. Director, Farmworker Legal Services of New York. 6/29/90.

Schoonmaker, Jack. Farmer. 8/8/90.

Segarra, Barbara. Deputy director, field operations, Rural Opportunities, Inc. 8/2/90.

Sibley, Charlotte. Attorney, Farmworker Legal Services of New York. 7/11/90, 7/7/93.

Simmons, Rev. Ivory. Community leader. 9/13/90.

Sorvello, Morris. Farmer. 8/1/90.

Tierno, Joseph A. Communications director, United Food and Commercial Workers, Local 1, and member, New York State Farm Minimum Wage Advisory Council. 7/6/90.

Turek, Dave. Farmer. 7/10/90.

Verbridge, Gerald. Farmer and member, New York State Farm Minimum Wage Advisory Council. 10/5/90.

Warren, G. Elliott. General manager, K. M. Davies Storage Co. 10/5/90.

Wright, Stephen R. Corporate vice president, procurement, Curtice Burns Foods. 9/14/90.

Young, Doug. Dairy farmer. 9/17/90.

Zimmerman, Paul R. Director of government relations, New York Farm Bureau. 8/6/90.

Anonymous interviews with farmworkers:
Middletown area, 8/9/90.
Wayne County, 9/13/90 and 11/2/90.
Hudson Valley, 10/16/90.

Arizona Interviews

Devereaux, Don. Journalist and former administrator, Maricopa County Organizing Project, and former press secretary, Arizona Farmworkers Union. 8/2/90.
Romney, K. Russell. General counsel, Arizona Agricultural Employment Relations Board. 7/11/90.
Thompson, Gary. Professor, Department of Agricultural Economics, University of Arizona. 6/13/90.
Wettstein, Nadine. Attorney, and former attorney, Southern Arizona Legal Aid. 7/5/90.

Florida Interviews

Barry, D. Marshall. Director of applied research, Center for Labor Research and Studies, Florida International University. 6/15/90.
Emerson, Robert D. Professor, Food and Resource Economics Department, University of Florida. 6/10/90.
Moreno, Tirso. General coordinator, Farmworker Association of Central Florida. 6/27/90, 6/11/93.
Perry, Roberta. Director, National Farmworker Ministry. 6/26/90.
Williams, Robert A. Attorney, Florida Rural Legal Services. 6/19/90.

New Jersey Interviews

Dominguez, Angel. Director of organizing, Comité Organizador de Trabajadores Agrícolas and former director, Comité de Apoyo a los Trabajadores Agrícolas. 7/11/90 and 11/2/90.
Goldberg, Richard. Attorney. 7/10/90.
Katz, Ira J. Staff attorney, International Ladies' Garment Workers' Union. 6/21/90.
Talbot, Keith. Senior attorney, Camden Regional Legal Services. 7/7/93.
Williams, Robert F. Professor of law, Rutgers University. 7/10/90, 8/21/90.

Ohio Interviews

W. K. Barger, Associate professor, Department of Anthropology, Indiana University, Indianapolis. 5/20/93.

Brooks, Ronald. General manager of agriculture, Heinz U.S.A. division, H. J. Heinz Co. 7/2/90.

Carroll, Harry. General manager, communications and labor relations, Heinz U.S.A. division, H. J. Heinz Co. 1/8/91.

Erven, Bernard L. Professor, Department of Agricultural Economics and Rural Sociology, Ohio State University. 5/22/90, 6/8/93.

Gallon, Jack. Attorney. 10/30/90.

Lucio, Benito. Migrant agricultural ombudsman for the state of Ohio. 6/15/90.

O'Brien, Jeremiah. Director, community relations, Campbell Soup Co. 11/20/90.

Rombach, Scott. Vice president, corporate relations, Campbell Soup Co. 11/20/90.

Velasquez, Baldemar. President, Farm Labor Organizing Committee. 7/24/90, 6/8/93.

Worcester, John. Litigation director, Advocates for Basic Legal Equality. 10/25/90.

Miscellaneous Interviews

Chertkov, Boren. Former general counsel, Agricultural Labor Relations Board. 5/27/93.

Cromer, Linda. Director of organizing, Retail, Wholesale and Department Store Union. 6/21/93.

Eisenbrey, Ross. Legislative director for U.S. Congressman William Ford, Democrat from Michigan. 6/29/90.

Glover, Robert W. Research associate, LBJ School of Public Administration, University of Texas, Austin. 10/22/90.

Goldstein, Bruce. Staff attorney, Farmworker Justice Fund, Inc. 6/15/90.

Greene, Joel. Economist, U.S. Department of Agriculture. 6/11/93.

Griffith, David. Associate scientist, Institute for Coastal and Marine Resources, and associate professor, Department of Sociology and Anthropology, East Carolina University. 6/9/93.

Gross, James A. Professor, New York State School of Industrial and Labor Relations, Cornell University. 5/26/93.

Haverkamp, Robert. Division of Foreign Labor Certification, U.S. Employment Service. 6/23/93.

Heppel, Monica. Assistant professor, Department of U.S. and Global Studies, Mount Vernon College. 6/9/93.

Hermanson, Jeff. Director of organizing, International Ladies' Garment Workers' Union. 6/14/93.

Mines, Richard. Agricultural economist, Office of the Assistant Secretary for Policy, U.S. Department of Labor. 6/3/93.

Rosenthal, Roger. Executive director, Migrant Legal Action Program. 6/15/90, 5/27/93.

Salins, Donald. Former assistant general counsel, Office of Representation Appeals, National Labor Relations Board. 6/4/93.

Schwartz, Bari. Legislative director for U.S. Congressman Howard Berman, Democrat from California. 6/25/90.

Subrin, Berton. Director, Office of Representation Appeals, National Labor Relations Board. 6/3/93.

Uehlein, Joseph. Executive assistant to president, Industrial Union Department, AFL-CIO. 6/21/93.

Vagley, Karen. Counsel for labor relations, U.S. House of Representatives Committee on Education and Labor. 6/26/90.

Valenta, Charlie. President, Local 1034, Retail, Wholesale and Department Store Union. 6/23/93.

Wial, Howard. Labor economist, International Labor Affairs Bureau, U.S. Department of Labor. 5/25/93.

Index

Administrative Procedure Act, 98
AFL, 80
AFL-CIO, 35, 40, 45, 91, 97
Agricultural Adjustment
    Administration, 30
Agricultural Labor Bureau, 46
Agricultural Labor Relations Act
    (ALRA): attempts to change, 43, 52;
    Gov. Edmund G. Brown, Jr., 41, 51,
    84; Gov. George Deukmejian, 52, 55,
    85; farm employers, 12, 51; farm
    labor contractors, 53, 77, 83; grower
    hostility to, 12, 43, 51, 52, 55; impact
    of, 53, 55, 82; and NLRA, 52, 82, 83,
    84; outside support for, 42, 43;
    politicization of, 84–85; provisions
    of, 49, 82–84; reasons for, 41–42; and
    secondary boycotts, 82; and UFW, 41,
    55, 84, 85; uniqueness of, 42, 49, 84
Agricultural Labor Relations Board
    (ALRB): bias of, 51–52, 55, 84–85;
    decisions of, 51–52, 82; elections and
    certifications, 42–43, 51, 55, 68, 84
Agricultural Producers Labor
    Committee, 46
Agricultural Workers Organizing
    Committee (AWOC), 35, 37, 38, 40
Alinsky, Saul, 36
American Hospital Association, 99
Antle, Bud, 38
Arizona, 9, 62–63
Arizona Agricultural Employment
    Relations Act, 62–63

Arizona Farm Workers Union, 63
Arkansas. *See* Southern Tenant Farmers'
    Union
Associated Farmers of California, 46
Aunt Jane's, 59, 87

bargaining rights: of American
    workers, 2; constitutional, 85–86; of
    farmworkers, 1–2, 12, 15, 62–63, 66,
    70, 81, 91, 103. *See also* Agricultural
    Labor Relations Act; National Labor
    Relations Act
benefits, fringe, 3–4, 21
Border Agricultural Workers Union, 67
boycotts: consumer, 37, 38, 41, 55, 59,
    69, 80; secondary, 82, 93, 97, 98
braceros, 32–35, 38
Brown, Edmund G., Jr., 41, 51, 84
Bush, George, 102

California: agricultural sector, 24, 25,
    41; collective bargaining laws in, 41,
    84 (*see also* Agricultural Labor
    Relations Act); farm labor, demand
    for, 19, 22, 24, 25–27; farm labor,
    supply of, 24, 72; farm labor activism
    in, 24, 27–28, 34, 41, 55; farm labor
    contractors in, 53–54, 76, 77; farm
    labor market, structure of, 19–20;
    farm labor strikes, 24, 28, 29, 36–37,
    63; farm union contracts in, 38, 53;
    farmworkers, discrimination against,
    13, 26, 27; farmworkers, foreign and

121